Gambling Culture

Editor: Tracy Biram

Volume 349

Independence Educational Publishers

First published by Independence Educational Publishers

The Studio, High Green

Great Shelford

Cambridge CB22 5EG

England

© Independence 2019

Copyright

Photocopy licence

ISBN-13: 978 1 86168 805 7

Printed in Great Britain

Zenith Print Group

Contents

Introduction

GAMBLING CULTURE is Volume 349 in the **ISSUES** series. The aim of the series is to offer current, diverse information about important issues in our world, from a UK perspective.

ABOUT GAMBLING CULTURE

Gambling addiction currently affects 430,000 people in the UK including around 25,000 children. From the National Lottery to horse racing, from video games to bingo, this book explores the trends in gambling. It also looks at the steps being taken to help people overcome their addiction.

It explores the work being done both in schools and via the media to educate people about the risks of gambling and the impact it can have on their lives, both socially and financially.

OUR SOURCES

Titles in the **ISSUES** series are designed to function as educational resource books, providing a balanced overview of a specific subject.

The information in our books is comprised of facts, articles and opinions from many different sources, including:

⇨ Newspaper reports and opinion pieces

⇨ Website factsheets

⇨ Magazine and journal articles

⇨ Statistics and surveys

⇨ Government reports

⇨ Literature from special interest groups.

A NOTE ON CRITICAL EVALUATION

Because the information reprinted here is from a number of different sources, readers should bear in mind the origin of the text and whether the source is likely to have a particular bias when presenting information (or when conducting their research). It is hoped that, as you read about the many aspects of the issues explored in this book, you will critically evaluate the information presented.

It is important that you decide whether you are being presented with facts or opinions. Does the writer give a biased or unbiased report? If an opinion is being expressed, do you agree with the writer? Is there potential bias to the 'facts' or statistics behind an article?

ASSIGNMENTS

In the back of this book, you will find a selection of assignments designed to help you engage with the articles you have been reading and to explore your own opinions. Some tasks will take longer than others and there is a mixture of design, writing and research-based activities that you can complete alone or in a group.

FURTHER RESEARCH

At the end of each article we have listed its source and a website that you can visit if you would like to conduct your own research. Please remember to critically evaluate any sources that you consult and consider whether the information you are viewing is accurate and unbiased.

Useful weblinks

www.bigissue.com

www.theconversation.com

www.gamcare.org.uk

www.gamblersanonymous.org.uk

www.gamblingcommission.gov.uk

www.gamblingtherapy.org

www.gordonmoody.org.uk

www.theguardian.com

www.independent.co.uk

www.inews.co.uk

www.lshtm.ac.uk

www.nhs.uk

www.parentzone.org.co.uk

www.telegraph.co.uk

www.yougov.co.uk

What is gambling?

In the Gambling Act 2005 gambling is defined as betting, gaming or participating in a lottery. That definition distinguishes between activities which need to be licensed and other activities which do not.

We categorise different gambling activities into what we call sectors:

⇨ Arcades (those for adults and those for families)

⇨ Betting (online, at an event or in a high street bookmakers)

⇨ Bingo (online or in a bingo hall)

⇨ Casino (online or in a casino)

⇨ Lotteries (raffles, tombolas, sweepstakes, etc.)

⇨ Gaming machines (fruit machines, fixed odds betting terminals, etc.)

Arcades

There are three types of amusement arcade:

⇨ adult gaming centres (AGCs)

⇨ licensed family entertainment centres (FECs)

⇨ unlicensed family entertainment centres (UFECs).

AGCs and FECs require a licence from the Gambling Commission. UFECs require a permit from the local licensing authority.

Gaming machines (fruit machines, slot machines) on arcade premises fall into different gaming machine categories depending on the levels of stake and prize offered.

Age restrictions for arcades

No one under the age of 18 is allowed to enter an AGC or the adults only area of a licensed FEC.

Betting

There are several different ways in which betting can be offered:

⇨ fixed odds betting

⇨ pool betting

⇨ acting as a betting intermediary

⇨ spread betting (regulated by the Financial Conduct Authority).

You need a licence from the Gambling Commission to offer betting services.

Fixed odds betting

The most common form of betting is fixed odds betting where you bet a stake to win a fixed amount calculated by the odds available. For example, a £10 bet at odds of 2/1 would return £30 (£20 of winnings + £10 stake) if successful. If unsuccessful you lose your £10 stake.

Fixed odds betting can be offered:

⇨ in betting shops (off-course)

⇨ on tracks (on-course)

⇨ by remote means (including online gambling).

Pool betting

Pool betting differs from fixed odds betting as winnings are determined by the sum of stakes paid into the pool. The amount you win is calculated by dividing the total pool (minus a commission fee for the organiser) by the number of winning tickets. Pool betting includes:

⇨ racecourse pool betting

⇨ football and other sports pool betting

⇨ fantasy football-type competitions.

The Tote (Successor Company) Limited holds the exclusive licence (until mid-2018) to offer pool betting in respect of GB horse racing. Tote can, however, give permission for a company to offer pool betting in respect of GB horse racing.

Betting intermediaries

A betting intermediary facilitates betting between two or more parties. They do not have liability for the bets but often take a commission fee from the winner. Betting intermediaries can be remote or non-remote.

Spread betting

We don't regulate spread betting. It is the responsibility of the Financial Conduct Authority.

Age restrictions for betting

No one under the age of 18 is allowed to bet with a licensed gambling business.

Bingo

What is bingo?

Although there is no legal definition of the game of bingo we have worked with the bingo industry to create an advice note: *What constitutes bingo*.

You need a licence from the Gambling Commission to offer bingo.

You can run bingo as a prize game without the need for a bingo operating licence in adult gaming centres, family entertainment centres, unlicensed family entertainment centres and travelling fairs.

Casinos

Casino games are available online or in casino premises.

Most casinos offer a variety of games, such as American roulette, punto banco (or baccarat) and blackjack. You can also play games of equal chance (such as poker) and gaming machines. A small number of casinos only offer electronic games and/or games of equal chance.

Lotteries

Raffles, tombolas and sweepstakes are all types of lottery.

Lotteries can only be run for good causes and cannot be run for commercial or private gain.

Large society lotteries and lotteries promoted by local authorities require a licence from the Gambling Commission.

Small society lotteries can operate under a registration with their local authority.

Other types of lottery do not require specific permission but there are rules that you must follow.

Age restrictions for lotteries

Lotteries differ from other types of gambling activity in that the minimum participation age is 16 for the National Lottery, society lotteries, customer lotteries and local authority lotteries, as opposed to 18 for other types of gambling. There is no minimum age requirement for other types of lotteries.

Gaming machines

What is a gaming machine (fruit machine, slot machine)?

A gaming machine is defined by the Gambling Act 2005 as a machine that is designed or adapted for use by individuals to gamble (whether or not it can also be used for other purposes). Most gaming machines are of the reel-based type, also known as fruit, slot or jackpot machines.

Several devices or systems are excluded from being defined as gaming machines including:

⇨ domestic or dual use computers

⇨ telephones or other machines for facilitating communication

⇨ machines designed or adapted to bet on future real events

⇨ lottery terminals

⇨ on a bingo premises, machines designed or adapted for the playing of bingo (including by way of prize gaming)

⇨ machines designed or adapted for the playing of bingo, by way of prize gaming, where a family entertainment centre gaming machine permit or a prize gaming permit is held

⇨ semi-automated casino games

⇨ fully-automated casino games.

What are gaming machine categories?

Gaming machines fall into categories depending on the maximum stake and prize available.

There is no statutory minimum percentage payout for gaming machines but all machines are required to clearly display the amounts paid to use the machine that is returned by way of prizes (described as the return to player (RTP) on the machine), or the odds of winning prizes from use of the machine.

Why do people gamble?

This question is often asked by relatives and friends as they cannot understand why gamblers are putting themselves and their loved ones through such pain and unhappiness. If something is causing such a problem, why not just stop and be happier? A similar question is 'why are some people able to gamble within their limits without developing such problems? Does it demonstrate a sign of weakness, or the inability to cope?' However, the truth of the matter is rarely so simple. Gambling problems are often experienced as being completely outside of the person's control, and 'just stopping' isn't felt to be a reasonable option.

Additionally, many people find themselves unable to explain why they continue to gamble despite the problems it causes in their day-to-day lives. The most obvious answer is 'for the money', but perhaps you can challenge yourself here: when you win, do you spend your winnings on more gambling? Do you continue to gamble until you have little or no money left?

A lot of gamblers feel they are waiting for the 'big win', which never comes but always seems tantalisingly close. But often, they find having a big win would simply fuel their desire for more gambling, leaving them feeling trapped into a behaviour with no way out. This would suggest that being 'in action' is the most important thing, rather than winning an amount of money. A big win can change gambling from entertainment to being about winning money. The problem here is that all forms of gambling have a house advantage meaning, over time, the house always wins. Or more importantly, the gambler always loses. This means any gambling you do that is driven by a need to win money, including trying to win back money you've already lost, is not going to work

Any entertainment can be a useful diversion from stress, grief or life's hassles but can turn negative when it stops being a diversion and starts being a way to cope. This is because ignoring a problem doesn't usually make it go away.

Using gambling to escape other problems can leave you with an even bigger problem, less money and less goodwill from family and friends.

There is another way of thinking about gambling, that it represents a symptom of a larger problem in life. While this might sound a bit scary to contemplate, perhaps consider whether you tend to gamble at certain times, or whether gambling is associated with certain feelings for you. It might well have played a large part in your life since you were quite young. If you think of it this way, you might realise that gambling problems are not a sign of weakness, but rather a way of coping with something bigger, in a way that on some level makes a lot of sense.

When gambling becomes a problem

It is very difficult to define when gambling becomes a problem. As it is different for everyone. If you, your family or friends think it might be causing issues in your life, then maybe it is time to rethink your gambling. There are many myths associated with gambling which include:

• *If I continue to gamble, I will win and therefore I can win back what I have lost*

• *Gambling is the only solution to my financial and other problems*

• *Gambling is the only way I can escape from stress.*

If gambling has stopped being fun for you and is starting to feel like a problem, you may find yourself asking why you gamble. But gambling doesn't start as a problem. However, gambling can change and grow without you noticing it becoming bigger in your life and that's where it can become a problem.

Why is it so hard to stop?

People who have gambling problems often ask themselves why they just can't stop. Even though there is no drug or substance involved in gambling, problem gambling is categorised as an addiction in the psychiatric literature in the same section as drug and alcohol addictions. That problem gambling is an addiction and has some of the same features in terms of brain activity as substance addictions explains why just trying to stop sometimes isn't enough to make it happen. It also explains why despite wanting to stop, many people will struggle to control their gambling and have to try many times to stop before being successful. It also explains why, just like with other types of addiction, some people will remain vulnerable to problems with gambling returning in the future.

www.gamblingtherapy.org

Gambling with our health: why the stakes don't get any higher

By Jacqui Thornton

A pair of handsome male celebrities invite me to click on a game based on their TV show, next to five glamorous young women promoting blackjack, and surrounded by animated slots with names such as Mega Moolah, Lotsa Loot and King Cashalot.

Welcome to the world of online gambling, where shiny young people appear to bet together for fun.

A few clicks away, there are more images: photos of eight young men, full of personality; one at the beach, another on a country walk, one playing the trombone in a band. Below the pictures are their names, dates of birth – and death.

All these men died by suicide as a direct result of gambling, according to their parents who have come together and founded the charity Gambling With Lives.

The men were all normal, bright, popular and happy with great futures ahead of them. Gambling was their only problem. They had not necessarily racked up massive debts – though some had – it was the insidious nature of what gambling had done to their hearts and their heads that caused their deaths, according to the charity.

Founders Liz and Charles Ritchie, whose son Jack took his own life last November aged 24 in Hanoi, Vietnam, say online gambling followed him wherever he went, with companies sending him inducements and invitations to play. Jack had been free from gambling for several months before his death – to be dragged back into the addiction proved too much for him. In his last letter, he wrote: 'Point is, I'm past the point of controlling myself and I'm not coming back from this one.'

The contrast of the images is not lost on Dr Heather Wardle, Assistant Professor at the London School of Hygiene & Tropical Medicine (LSHTM), who specialises in gambling behaviour, policy and practice, and Gerda Reith, Professor of Social Sciences at the University of Glasgow, who have been collaborating on creating a definition of gambling-related harms to be used in British policy and practice.

Prof. Reith said: 'The idea of holding up this ideal of gambling to win money, to make life a little bit better and more exciting to people who often have very little money to start with, when what more often happens is that they end up losing money, getting into debt, and everything actually gets a lot worse – it's tragic. There's a huge human, as well as social and economic, cost to this.'

Concern over problem gambling is a hot topic. In November 2018 the Gambling Commission, which regulates gambling providers, revealed that 1.7% of children are classed as having a gambling problem.

The Commission's study suggested that 14% – equivalent to 450,000 – children aged 11 to 16 bet regularly, more than have taken drugs, smoked or drunk alcohol.

'There's a huge human, as well as social and economic, cost to this.'

Prof. Gerda Reith

Prevalence of gambling in the UK among 11–16-year-olds in 2018

14% had gambled in the previous week

2.2% are 'at risk'

1.7% are defined as problem gamblers

Shortly before the release of that report, there had been renewed concern over the harm caused by Fixed Odds Betting Terminals (FOBTs), electronic gambling machines found in betting shops where punters can bet £100 stakes every few seconds. The roulette versions have been dubbed the 'crack cocaine' of gambling.

The Government was forced into an embarrassing climbdown over cutting stakes on FOBTs from £100 to £2 in April rather than October 2019 – the delay of which sports minister Tracey Crouch had resigned over two weeks before.

For it is the Department for Digital, Culture, Media & Sport that is responsible for gambling. Many now argue it is not a sporting or leisure problem, but a health issue. The Labour Party's deputy leader Tom Watson MP said recently that problem gambling is a hidden epidemic and must be treated as a public health emergency.

This was welcomed by Dr Wardle. She believes the widespread harms of gambling, not just for the individual taking part but their families and wider society, have been hidden for too long. It is, she says, disruptive and extremely challenging.

But because its harms are not currently quantified, it's easy for policy makers not to take the consequences of problem gambling seriously enough.

She says there's a sense that people get into problems, lose a bit of money and it's considered their own fault, an individual's problem with no understanding of the severe and wider nature of the consequences.

Dr Wardle said: 'Until you have more of that recognition, you don't get adequate policy responses, or a strategic approach from government as to what you're going to do on this issue because there is, arguably, a tendency to err on the side of protection of people's liberty to engage with this activity, rather than prevention.'

Prof Reith agrees. 'An individual with gambling problems undoubtedly needs help from professionals, but we also need to look at the knock-on effects on their families, their relationships, on debt,' she said.

'Debt has massive ripple effects in the economy. At the extreme end it can tear families apart, people can lose their homes. On a lesser scale, it means relationships and trust can be eroded, kids go without that school trip, or that extra Christmas present. The erosion of money and of trust just makes life that bit harder and more difficult.'

These ripple effects can be extensive and enduring. She adds: 'These things don't just go away after the gambling's cleared up, so to speak. The broken relationships, the credit default, and maybe the criminal activity that people engage in. Whether it's borrowing money off friends that they never pay back, or defrauding their work – these things have long-term impact.'

Earlier this year as deputy chair of the Responsible Gambling Strategy Board, Dr Wardle led an expert group with Prof. Reith and others to propose a formal definition of gambling-related harms.

The resulting document published in July, *Measuring gambling-related harms: A Framework For Action* stated 'gambling-related harms are the adverse impacts from gambling on the health and wellbeing of individuals, families, communities and society'. It sounds simple, but the authors say it's needed to encourage a change in the way policy makers, politicians and wider society think about gambling in this country.

There have been positive responses from the Gambling Commission, people who work with problem gamblers, and problem gamblers themselves. Government has been less vocal, but Dr Wardle is cautiously hopeful the message is getting through. Public Health England, she says, has been charged to think about problem gambling, with proposals for a cross-departmental group between the Department of Health and Social Care and the Department of Culture, Media and Sport. 'There are positive conversations happening with the NHS,' she said. 'There's going to be small incremental changes which hopefully over time will add up to something bigger.'

The expert group will next explore the impacts on young people specifically and attempt to estimate the cost of gambling-related harms to society and the economy.

Gambling over time

It is instructive to look at how gambling has been perceived by society and treated by the medical profession in comparison with alcohol and drugs, which have become such significant public health issues in the UK.

They have long been lumped together. At the beginning of the last century, Joseph Rowntree, the founder of the

Joseph Rowntree Foundation social policy charity, identified gambling as one of seven social evils (the others being poverty, war, slavery, intemperance, opium and impurity).

Much of the criticism was moralistic and quasi-religious in tone, wringing hands over poor people wasting their money when they should be working hard and saving. The same criticisms were used by the temperance movement – drinking was bad, but especially when the poor did it.

Around this time, the idea developed that excessive alcohol use was a disease to be treated. This was partly because of the development of the medical profession and specialities including 'inebriety' – the term used to describe the disease where someone was inebriated, due to alcohol or drugs.

Prof. Virginia Berridge, a social historian at the London School of Hygiene & Tropical Medicine, says many doctors were frustrated by the 'revolving door' of excessive drinkers being criminalised for being drunk and disorderly and thrown into prison for a month, only to be released and repeat their behaviour.

'The only way they could change things for the better was to establish a disease view of the use of alcohol to excess so they could introduce a treatment structure,' she says.

During the First World War the word 'addiction' started to be used over concerns about cocaine in the West End of London, and 'alcoholism' became the preferred term for excessive alcohol use.

In the 1950s, the term 'habituation' was used by the World Health Organization (WHO) to describe being accustomed to illicit drugs rather than addicted, and then in the 1970s and 1980s 'dependence' was introduced by the WHO as a concept to unify alcohol, drugs and smoking.

> *'Gambling, and the marketing of gambling, has become really normalised and accessible. This is unsustainable and is causing harm, particularly to vulnerable groups.'*
>
> *Prof. Gerda Reith*

It was around this time that gambling first became included in this arena in the UK. One of the pioneering centres of research on dependence was the Addiction Research Unit at London's Institute of Psychiatry, where psychologist Jim Oford worked. He wrote *Excessive Appetites*, one of the first academic discussions that discussed gambling, alongside the usual 'addictions' as well as eating excessively and sexual activity.

'Psychology as a discipline was very important in broadening the idea of what was a compulsive behaviour that people were doing against their own best interests,' says Prof. Berridge.

In modern times, according to Prof. Reith, problem gambling has been medicalised as a psychological flaw; a mental health problem that affected individuals who were supposedly too impulsive to control themselves. It was incorporated into the American Psychiatric Association's internationally used *Diagnostic Manual of Psychiatric Disorders* in those terms in the 1980s.

The early edition used the term 'pathological' gambling but in 2013 it was changed to 'gambling disorder' and placed in the category of behavioural addictions.

Social scientists and others believe that following this medical model overlooks the much more extensive and unseen harms that widespread gambling can cause.

Legislation and liberalisation

Despite this increased recognition from the academic community, Dr Wardle finds it interesting that during the 20th century, while alcohol and drugs remained problems that society was concerned about, there has been 'collective amnesia' about gambling, which was hidden away in the back streets through strict regulation.

This changed once successive governments liberalised the laws. The introduction of the National Lottery in 1994 paved the way for the 2005 Gambling Act. Once the act came into force in 2007, gambling was more visible through open advertising; putting it online made the activity even more prominent and available. Prof. Reith says the new act was framed as a modernising of attitudes in line with new technologies, but in fact politicians have permitted more and more intense and hard forms of gambling and allowed it to be widely promoted. 'First of all into casinos, and then out of casinos into the high street, onto the internet,' she said. 'Gambling, and the marketing of gambling, has become really normalised and accessible. This is unsustainable and is causing harm, particularly to vulnerable groups.'

Dr Wardle does not believe the public was clamouring for liberalisation of gambling in the early 2000s. 'It was a really deliberate attempt by those in power to reposition gambling,' she says. The pendulum has now swung: today's Labour Party has vowed to create a new Gambling Act with prevention of harm as a core value.

Rise in gambling advertising

234,000 ads   **1.39 million ads**

2007 ⬆ **2012**

600% increase in gambling advertising on TV since the 2005 Gambling Act came into force in 2007

The legislators in 2005 were likely to have been influenced by Australia, where electronic gaming machines had been introduced in the late 1980s. The country soon became dependent on gambling as a form of state finance. Martin McKee, Professor of European Public Health at the London School of Hygiene & Tropical Medicine, says that's why better regulation – limiting the appeal of gambling – is needed to prevent it ever becoming a taxation cash cow in the UK.

'There's a real danger with what are called sin taxes, in that you get dependent on them,' he says. And then you have a conflict of interest because you're happy to see the activity go on because you're generating money for public health.

Counting the cost of gambling

But before government commits to funding prevention strategies in the UK, the problem needs to be quantified. Dr Wardle sees a particular parallel with alcohol in that most people drink, many enjoy it, but some will get into difficulties.

The difference is that the harms are much more visible. People attend hospital with issues from drinking and there are records of deaths related to alcoholic-related liver disease, which can be quantified. With gambling, both the activity and the harms are hidden. GPs may see patients with poor physical health and mental health issues and have no idea that gambling is underpinning the symptoms.

And while suicide is a shocking way of linking gambling with deaths, Dr Wardle believes we have no way of knowing how many other deaths are indirectly associated.

She said: 'We've got no assessment of gambling-related morbidity and that, for me, is crucial. It may well not be at the same level of alcohol, but that doesn't make this any less of a public health challenge.'

Prof. Reith believes there are similarities between gambling and tobacco, alcohol and fast food, and she draws the link in her new book *Addictive Consumption: Capitalism, Modernity and Excess*. In the same way we are used to the concept of obesogenic and alcogenic environments, she believes we now live in an 'aleatory' environment, from the Latin 'to gamble', in which gambling is pervasive and widespread.

She says in the colonial era, sugar, tea, coffee and tobacco were seen as deeply problematic, likened to drugs and often criticised, regulated or outlawed. 'As they became sources of massive profit and revenue, they were liberalised, accepted and normalised,' she said. 'There are some similar trends going on with gambling.'

But waves of acceptance, she says, eventually go full cycle and today, a focus on health risks has stimulated increasing regulation again. Now there's an understanding that consumption of certain things such as sugar, tobacco or alcohol brings problems in terms of obesity and cancers and addictions.

> *'We've got no assessment of gambling-related morbidity and that, for me, is crucial. It may well not be at the same level of alcohol, but that doesn't make this any less of a public health challenge.'*
>
> *Dr Heather Wardle*

According to Prof. Reith, there's also increasing awareness of industry tactics: the production and marketing of potentially dangerous forms of consumption is driven by the profit motive, and politicians are often lobbied by those industries in ways that mean they often avoid state regulation.

The other comparison with food is that it's not just whether you eat it, it's how you eat it. With gambling, there's a sliding scale of potential harm, with lotteries considered the 'soft' forms and electronic gaming machines and online slots 'hard'.

But it's not only that some types are intrinsically less harmful. Harm depends on the frequency and speed at which people play certain games; the amounts of time and money they lose, and on how their losses affect other people.

All types of gambling, she says, have the potential to be harmful if you can't afford the losses. 'Gambling isn't necessarily harmful in itself, it's losses relative to income that's important.'

Prevalence of gambling in the UK (2010)

73% of the adult population (16+) gamble

56% excluding the National Lottery

14% of the adult population gamble online

Who is harmed the most?

In order to provide prevention and treatment strategies, it's important to know who's at risk. Anybody can develop a gambling problem, but like other public health issues, it is 'socially patterned': people who live in more economically deprived circumstances are all more likely to experience harm.

This is because loss of money affects poor people the most. Gambling problems are far more intensive when people are living on the breadline. From a public health perspective, gambling is very much an activity that reinforces health and social inequalities.

Surveys of gambling behaviour consistently show two to three times more men are problem gamblers than women, but Dr Wardle believes this could be because the clinical criteria and definitions of problem gambling were originally based on conversations with men.

Women do choose to gamble in different ways from men, and traditionally it was thought that women preferred games of chance such as the lottery, scratch cards or fruit machines, whereas men choose games of skill such as betting or poker. Prof. Wardle questioned this theory in her PhD.

'There is no biological reason that women choose a game of chance over a game of skill. It is completely socially conditioned," she says. "When the legislation on bookmakers was introduced in the 1960s, the politicians created deliberately austere, unlikable places to try and put women off going to them. Bingo halls were put in places women already went, such as former cinemas.'

The fact that women do enjoy skilled gambling activities was shown in World Cup betting statistics, which included more bets from women this year. Dr Wardle said: 'It seems entirely obvious to me that if you change the circumstances in which gambling is provided – and you now have online gambling where women can do it in a sort of safe space – then of course women are going to be engaged."

Young people are also an at-risk group and the risk of harm is increasing. The Gambling Commission 2018 report says 1.7% of 11–16-year-olds are problem gamblers, compared with 0.9% in 2017, and 2.2% 'at risk', up from 1.3% in 2017.

According to Dr Wardle's latest published research problems among young people may be underestimated.

This generation is growing up with a fundamentally altered relationship to gambling and a fundamentally altered relationship to technology. Because gambling happens in cyberspace it is particularly attractive to them.

As a result, her current area of research, backed by a Wellcome Fellowship, is to understand youth gambling behaviour and its relationship with changing technology.

She's currently recruiting 14–18-year-old school children for focus groups and doing indepth interviews with 30 young online betters, mapping how technology has shaped their gambling career, followed by a survey of 14- to 24-year-olds.

Cyberspace and mobile gambling

The ability to gamble on mobile phones has caused another radical change. The recent Gambling Commission study showed 13% of 11–16-year-olds have ever played online gambling-style games (which are often free to play and offer no cash prizes), with more than half of these (54%) playing via apps on smartphones or tablets.

Smartphones can be addictive in their own right; and when appealing technology is embedded on an appealing device enabling an appealing activity such as gambling, Prof Reith believes it's creating a perfect storm.

'A lot of policy circles are still coming to terms with the fact that gambling happens on the internet,' says Prof. Reith. 'Actually the biggest growing sector is mobile, and there's very little research on this.'

She believes mobile technologies make gambling more immediate, more intense, and a lot more personal. 'This device that I can hold in my hand and take everywhere with me, is also the device I can gamble on. And it's not just the device that I see gambling on, I also gamble through it as it holds my bank details.

'It's very immersive and of course it's going to be hugely appealing for the generation who've grown up with these things.'

December 2018

Designed to deceive: how gambling distorts reality and hooks your brain

An article from **The Conversation.**

THE CONVERSATION

By Mike Robinson, Assistant Professor of Psychology, Wesleyan University

To call gambling a 'game of chance' evokes fun, random luck and a sense of collective engagement. These playful connotations may be part of why almost 80 per cent of American adults gamble at some point in their lifetime. When I ask my psychology students why they think people gamble, the most frequent suggestions are for pleasure, money or the thrill.

While these might be reasons why people gamble initially, psychologists don't definitely know why, for some, gambling stops being an enjoyable diversion and becomes compulsive. What keeps people playing even when it stops being fun? Why stick with games people know are designed for them to lose? Are some people just more unlucky than the rest of us, or simply worse at calculating the odds?

As an addiction researcher for the past 15 years, I look to the brain to understand the hooks that make gambling so compelling. I've found that many are intentionally hidden in how the games are designed. And these hooks work on casual casino-goers just as well as they do on problem gamblers.

Uncertainty as its own reward in the brain

One of the hallmarks of gambling is its uncertainty – whether it's the size of a jackpot or the probability of winning at all. And reward uncertainty plays a crucial role in gambling's attraction.

Dopamine, the neurotransmitter the brain releases during enjoyable activities such as eating, sex and drugs, is also released during situations where the reward is uncertain. In fact, dopamine release increases particularly during the moments leading up to a potential reward. This anticipation effect might explain why dopamine release parallels an individual's levels of gambling 'high' and the severity of his or her gambling addiction. It likely also plays a role in reinforcing the risk-taking behaviour seen in gambling.

Studies have shown that the release of dopamine during gambling occurs in brain areas similar to those activated by taking drugs of abuse. In fact, similar to drugs, repeated exposure to gambling and uncertainty produces lasting changes in the human brain. These reward pathways, similar to those seen in individuals suffering from drug addiction, become hypersensitive. Animal studies suggest that these brain changes due to uncertainty can even enhance gamblers' cravings and desire for addictive drugs.

Repeated exposure to gambling and uncertainty can even change how you respond to losing. Counterintuitively, in individuals with a gambling problem, losing money comes to trigger the rewarding release of dopamine almost to the same degree that winning does. As a result, in problem gamblers, losing sets off the urge to keep playing, rather than the disappointment that might prompt you to walk away, a phenomenon known as chasing losses.

Lights and sounds egg you on

But gambling is more than just winning and losing. It can be a whole immersive environment with an array of flashing lights and sounds. This is particularly true in a busy casino, but even a game or gambling app on a smartphone includes plenty of audio and visual frills to capture your attention.

But are they just frills? Studies suggest that these lights and sounds become more attractive and capable of triggering urges to play when they are paired with reward uncertainty. In particular, win-associated cues – such as jingles that vary in length and size as a function of jackpot size – both increase excitement and lead gamblers to overestimate how often they are winning. Crucially, they can also keep you gambling longer and encourage you to play faster.

Feeling like a winner while you're losing

Since games of chance are set up so the house always has an advantage, a gambler wins infrequently at best. You might only rarely experience the lights and sounds that come along with hitting a true jackpot. However, the gaming industry may have devised a way to overcome that issue.

Over the last few decades, casinos and game manufacturers significantly upgraded slot machines, retiring the old mechanical arms and reels in favour of electronic versions known as electronic gaming machines. These new computerised games and online slots come with more attractive colourful lights and a variety of sounds. They also possess more reels, ushering in a new era of multi-line video slot machines. Having multiple lines enables players to place a bunch of bets per spin, often up to 20 or more. Although each individual bet can be small, many players place the maximum number of bets on each spin. This strategy means a player can win on some lines while losing on others, netting less than the original wager. Even when you 'win', you don't come out ahead, a phenomenon known as 'losses disguised as wins'. Yet each win, even when it is a loss disguised as a win, comes with the lights and sounds of victory.

The result is that these multi-line slot machines produce more enjoyment and are highly preferred by players. Crucially, they tend to make gamblers overestimate how often they're truly winning. The dramatic increase in the frequency of wins, whether real or fabricated, produces more arousal and activation of reward pathways in the brain, possibly accelerating the rate at which brain changes occur. Multi-line slots also seem to promote the development of 'dark flow', a trance-like state in which players get wholly absorbed in the game, sometimes for hours on end.

Almost: near-miss effect and chasing your losses

The rise of electronic gambling machines also means that rather than being constrained by the physical arrangement of different possible outcomes on each reel, possible outcomes are programmed onto a set of virtual reels. Gaming designers can therefore stack the deck to make certain events occur more frequently than others.

This includes near-misses, where one of the reels stops just short of lining up for a jackpot. These near-miss almost-wins recruit areas of the brain that usually respond to wins, and increase one's desire to play more, especially in problem gamblers.

This phenomenon is not confined to slot machines and casinos. Near-misses play an integral part in the addictive potential of smartphone games like the very popular *Candy Crush*.

Near-misses are more arousing than losses – despite being more frustrating and significantly less pleasant than missing by a longshot. But crucially, almost winning triggers a more substantial urge to play than even winning itself. Near-misses seem to be highly motivating and increase player commitment to a game, resulting in individuals playing longer than they intended. The size of the dopamine response to a near-miss in fact correlates with the severity of an individual's gambling addiction.

Gambling and its games

When you engage in recreational gambling, you are not simply playing against the odds, but also battling an enemy trained in the art of deceit and subterfuge. Games of chance have a vested interest in hooking players for longer and letting them eventually walk away with the impression they did better than chance, fostering a false impression of skill.

For many people, these carefully designed outcomes enhance the satisfaction they get from gambling. It may remain easy for them to simply walk away when the chips run out.

But gambling isn't only a lighthearted promise of a good time and a possible jackpot. Up to two per cent of the US population are problem gamblers, suffering from what's recently been reclassified as gambling disorder.

It stands out as one of the few addictions that doesn't involve consumption of a substance, such as a drug. Like other forms of addiction, gambling disorder is a solitary and isolating experience. It's tied to growing anxiety, and problem gamblers are at greater risk of suicide.

For these more susceptible individuals, the game designers' hooks start to seem more sinister. A solution to life's problems always feels just one spin away.

13 August 2018

Gambling participation in 2017: behaviour, awareness and attitudes

An extract from the annual report.

Headline findings

45% Percentage of people who have participated in any form of gambling in the past four weeks

(48% in year to December 2016)

31% Percentage of people who have participated in gambling in the past four weeks, excluding those who had only played the National Lottery draw

(33% in year to December 2016)

18% Percentage of people who had gambled online in the past four weeks

(17% in year to December 2016)

1% Percentage of people who had played on machines in a bookmakers in the past four weeks

(1% in year to December 2016)

0.8% Proportion of respondents who were identified as problem gamblers

According to the full PGSI or DSM-IV screen

3.9% Proportion of respondents who were identified as low or moderate-risk gamblers

According to the full PGSI or DSM-IV screen

51% Proportion of online gamblers who have gambled using a mobile phone or tablet

(43% in year to December 2016)

26% Proportion of online gamblers who have bet in-play

(26% in year to December 2016)

6% Proportion of gamblers who have ever self-excluded

(6% in year to December 2016)

33% Proportion of people who think that gambling is fair and can be trusted

(34% in year to December 2016)

41% Proportion of people who think that gambling is associated with crime

(39% in year to December 2016)

Survey findings

Gambling participation

Our research found that overall, gambling participation has decreased since 2016 with 45% of people aged 16+ having participated in at least one form of gambling in the past four weeks in 2017 (48% in 2016). Men are more likely to have gambled than women and those aged 55–64 are most likely to have gambled in the past four weeks.

This is predominantly driven by participation in the National Lottery draws as when people who have only gambled in the National Lottery draws are excluded, participation is highest among 16–34-year-olds.

Overall, 18% of people have gambled online in the past four weeks. Those aged 25–34 and 55–64 have seen the largest increases in online gambling participation whereas those aged 16–24 have seen a decline in online gambling participation in 2017. In terms of gambling activities:

⇨ The National Lottery draws remain the most popular gambling activity, followed by scratchcards and other lotteries.

⇨ Football and horse racing are the most popular betting activities.

⇨ All gambling activities have seen an increase in online participation with the exception of betting on horse races and spread betting.

⇨ In-person participation has declined for most activities.

Problem gambling estimates

An estimated 0.8% of people were identified as a problem gambler according to the full Problem Gambling Severity Index (PGSI)2 or DSM-IV screen with a further 3.9% identifying as at low or moderate risk.

Online gambling behaviour

Although declining in use for gambling, laptops remain the most popular method of accessing online gambling in 2017 with 50% of online gamblers using a laptop. The use of mobile phones has seen the largest increase to 39% (an increase of ten percentage points). The majority of online gamblers (97%) play at home. Male online gamblers were more likely than females to gamble outside of the home including on their commute, at work, at a venue or in a pub/club – as were younger age groups. Among online gamblers, 27% have bet in-play, with rates highest in 25–34-year-olds but the largest increase was seen in 55–64-year-olds. On average, online gamblers have four accounts with online gambling operators. 6% of online gamblers have bet on eSports during the past 12 months, with rates highest among 25–34-year-olds.

Consumer analysis

Awareness of self-exclusion among those who have never excluded remains stable at 35%. Overall, 6% of gamblers have ever self-excluded. Men and those aged 25–34 are most likely to self-exclude. Among gamblers, 60% have either seen or received gambling-related information from a gambling operator, with most having seen or received

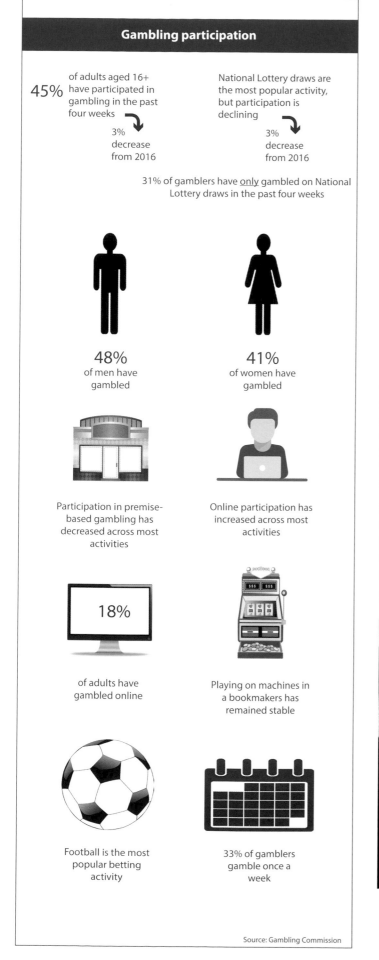

Gambling participation

45% of adults aged 16+ have participated in gambling in the past four weeks

3% decrease from 2016

National Lottery draws are the most popular activity, but participation is declining

3% decrease from 2016

31% of gamblers have only gambled on National Lottery draws in the past four weeks

48% of men have gambled

41% of women have gambled

Participation in premise-based gambling has decreased across most activities

Online participation has increased across most activities

18% of adults have gambled online

Playing on machines in a bookmakers has remained stable

Football is the most popular betting activity

33% of gamblers gamble once a week

Source: Gambling Commission

---

information relating to transaction and play history of their account.

Overall, 22% have read terms and conditions, of which 27% felt they had been in a situation where terms and conditions had been unfair. Overall, 8% of gamblers have ever made a complaint to or about a gambling operator, with rates highest among 18–24-year-olds.

In terms of social media and advertising:

⇨ 26% of online gamblers follow a gambling company on a social media platform with rates highest among 18–24-year-olds.

⇨ Facebook remains the most popular social media platform on which online gamblers follow gambling companies.

⇨ 51% of people have seen a gambling advert on the television in the past week and 46% of people have seen or heard a gambling sponsorship on the television or radio in the past week.

⇨ Online gamblers are more likely to be prompted to spend money on gambling by advertising (e.g. seeing an advert on television) than social media posts.

Perceptions and attitudes

Overall, perceptions and attitudes towards gambling are more negative than in 2016 with 33% of respondents thinking that gambling is fair and can be trusted and 41% thinking that gambling is associated with criminal activity. Theft and fraud are the crimes people associate the most with gambling.

In addition, 80% of people think there are too many opportunities for gambling nowadays and 71% think that gambling is dangerous for family life; however, 64% of respondents thought that people should have the right to gamble whenever they want.

February 2018

www.gov.uk

Problem gambling among sportsmen reaches 'crisis' point

By Ben Rumsby

Problem gambling in football and other sports has reached 'crisis' point and bookmakers must do more to prevent it, experts will warn on Thursday at the launch of a major drive to boost awareness of its life-threatening consequences.

With the surge in referrals for treatment of sports people with an out-of-control betting habit showing no sign of abating, the Professional Players Federation and GambleAware have come together to create a self-help tool aimed specifically at the industry's biggest stars.

The PPF, which represents elite footballers, rugby players, cricketers and other top sportsmen and women – will also urge 'responsible bookmakers' to ensure sponsorship agreements with a sport include provision for mandatory education for participants about the risks of problem gambling.

The wake-up call comes three years after the PPF published alarming research which found professional sportspeople were three times more likely than the general public to develop the crippling compulsion.

It also comes seven months since *The Daily Telegraph* launched its 'Sports Mental Health Crisis' campaign after Prince Harry sparked a national debate by revealing in an exclusive interview he had sought counselling over the death of his mother.

The Sporting Chance Clinic, famed for treating sportspeople with alcohol or drug-related conditions, has in recent years seen the vast majority of those seeking help do so for problem gambling, which, it is claimed, has the highest suicide rate of any addiction.

A new website, www.ppf.org.uk/pg, will be officially unveiled on Thursday during GambleAware's fifth annual Harm-Minimisation Conference at The King's Fund in London. The site includes films featuring powerful testimonies from former Premier League players Clarke Carlisle and John Hartson, and former professional Scott Davies, each of whom has battled the addiction and who open up about its devastating effects.

Marc Etches, the GambleAware chief executive, said: 'The relationship between sport and gambling is at a crisis. Gambling-related advertising and promotion is embedded in professional sport generally, and football in particular. We're delighted to fund this important initiative, which has enabled the PPF to take a proactive stance, helping

to educate professional players about the risks and encouraging those who may already be struggling with a gambling problem to talk about it and seek help. This isn't a job for the PPF alone, and we're keen to see more clubs think more deeply about the impact of gambling-related harm on their players and fans alike.'

The chairman of the PPF, West Bromwich Albion icon Brendon Batson, added: 'Many player associations are already doing excellent gambling education for their players but, as the gambling environment evolves, we are looking at new ways of engaging with the players. Thanks to GambleAware, we have created a world-leading resource for professional athletes about problem gambling. Everyone needs to be aware of their duty of care to players when it comes to gambling.'

Key findings

⇨ Research published by the PPF three years ago found professional sportspeople were three times more likely than non-sportspeople to become problem gamblers.

⇨ The same study, which surveyed professional footballers and cricketers, estimated at least 192 of them suffered from gambling problems, with a further 440 at risk of doing so.

⇨ More than a quarter of respondents to the survey said industry sponsorship had an impact on problem gambling, and nearly one in three thought betting firms 'encouraged' sportspeople to bet.

⇨ According to a recent report by the Gambling Commission, more than two million people in the UK are either problem gamblers or at risk of addiction.

⇨ Almost half of Premier League clubs (nine) now have a betting firm as their shirt sponsor, with 16 teams in the Championship and League One having similar deals.

⇨ 95 per cent of television advertising breaks during live UK football matches feature at least one gambling advert.

⇨ Approximately seven out of ten referrals to the Sporting Chance Clinic are for gambling-related issues.

The website and films do not tell sportspeople not to gamble but provide guidelines on minimising their risk of becoming an addict while doing so. They include: being sober and in a good mood; setting limits on time spent betting and the amount of money wagered; and keeping a record of winnings and losses. They also warn against chasing losses, a trap highly-competitive sportspeople are particularly at risk of falling into.

Three years ago, the PPF published a study of almost 350 footballers and cricketers. One in ten respondents said they gambled to 'fit in', one in four said they were encouraged by team-mates to do it, even more said industry sponsorship had an impact on problem gambling, and nearly one in three thought betting firms 'encouraged' sportspeople to bet.

The links between sport and bookmakers have grown in recent years, with almost half of Premier League clubs sporting gambling logos on their shirts – something Labour recently announced it would ban if it came to power. Virtually all teams now have an 'official betting partner', while the English Football League recently extended Sky Bet's title sponsorship of its three divisions by another five years.

A study found 95 per cent of television advertising breaks during UK football matches featured at least one gambling advert, a decade after the law was changed to relax restrictions on such adverts. The Football Association did decide this summer to cut all commercial ties with betting firms but that was due to a perceived conflict of interest with its role as a regulator – including policing its blanket ban on gambling on the game itself.

Sporting Chance chief executive Colin Bland says in one of the films released on Thursday: 'Sportspeople have time; it's a stressful place; many time[s] away from home; and gambling's easy. The other thing that sportspeople tend to have is they think that they've got a little bit of expertise, that they can beat the system. I think it's a cocktail that creates a perfect storm, that if I'm a sportsperson that might have emotional problems, that gambling is the choice of what I might use to fix me.'

6 December 2017

Online betting companies boosted by new gamblers during World Cup

James Mundell, Director, YouGovConsumer Research

New YouGov custom research underlines how important the World Cup has been in attracting new customers to betting companies.

YouGov's research reveals how the scale of excitement and enthusiasm generated by the tournament has translated into involvement into betting, whether that was in a fun office-based competition, or with an established betting organisation.

The study shows that 14% of Brits (around seven million people) took part in a World Cup sweepstake with their friends, family or workplace, including almost a quarter (24%) of full-time workers.

Outside of the work environment, YouGov data suggests that six million people in the UK placed a bet on the tournament, either in a traditional high-street betting shop, or online (equivalent to 12% of the adult population). Crucially for online brands, more than three times as many people placed their bet online than in a physical bookmaker.

The exciting element of this for betting brands – aside from the general willingness to gamble on the competition – is that more than one million of these people were 'new gamblers', i.e. they had not placed a bet on sport in the previous year.

Introductory offers have sometimes been derided by industry critics. But their importance can't be overestimated in this case. One-third of World Cup bettors (around two million people) opened up a new account in order to take advantage of free bets and offers.

The challenge for gambling brands is to sustain interest in the industry now that the hope and hype of the tournament has dissipated. With the next World Cup an agonising four years away, gambling companies can't rely on the 'Three Lions' to bring customers in, so marketing campaigns concentrated on new but infrequent consumers are crucial.

23 July 2018

www. yougov.co.uk

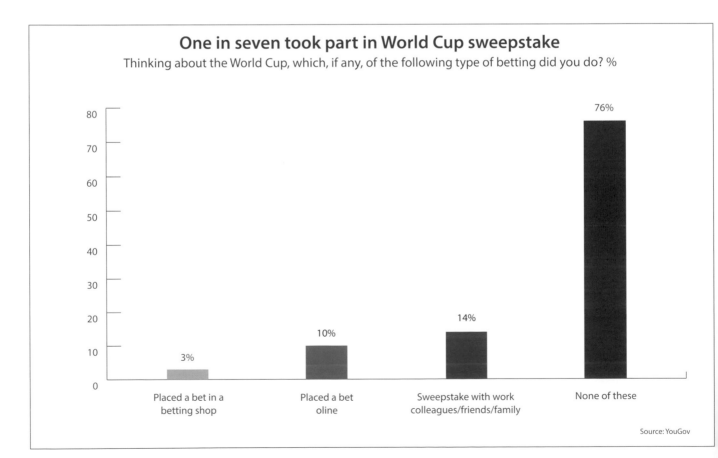

One in seven took part in World Cup sweepstake

Thinking about the World Cup, which, if any, of the following type of betting did you do? %

- Placed a bet in a betting shop: 3%
- Placed a bet oline: 10%
- Sweepstake with work colleagues/friends/family: 14%
- None of these: 76%

Source: YouGov

Number of problem gamblers aged 11–16 rises to 55,000

Quadrupling of figure in two years branded 'generational scandal' and blamed on TV ads and smartphone apps.

The quadrupling of child problem gamblers to more than 50,000 in two years has been branded a 'generational scandal'.

A Gambling Commission audit due for release on Wednesday reveals that the number of problem gamblers aged 11 to 16 rose to 55,000 over two years. It also found that 70,000 youngsters were at risk and that 450,000 children bet regularly, the equivalent of one in seven children aged 11 to 16.

The audit, reported in the *Daily Mail,* said the youngsters were staking an average of £16 a week on fruit machines, bingo, betting shops and online games, which are all illegal for under-18s.

The findings were branded 'deeply concerning' by the Church of England, which warned that the country needed to take the 'dangers of gambling seriously'.

The bishop of St Albans, the Right Reverend Alan Smith, branded the findings that 55,000 children were classed as problem gamblers as a 'generational scandal'.

He added: 'Today's findings by the Gambling Commission make worrying reading and serve as a warning to parents. After years of progress, it seems the rates of children gambling are creeping back up. These figures suggest 450,000 11- to 16-year-olds have gambled in the past week – that is deeply concerning. We need to start taking the dangers of gambling seriously.' The audit also revealed that children were being inundated with gambling adverts, with two-thirds telling the auditors they had seen them on TV. It said close to a million young people had been exposed to gambling through 'loot boxes' in video games or on smartphone apps. Loot boxes are chance-based items that can be purchased in video games to win prizes and have been likened to poker machines.

The audit found that more children said they had placed a bet in the past week than drank alcohol, smoked or taken drugs.

Smith said the Government, local authorities, schools and charities needed to put in place more safeguards to protect children from becoming problem gamblers.

'However much the gambling industry says it is not targeting the young, it is clear that a significant minority of teenagers are still being drawn into gambling and it is no coincidence that one in six children have seen gambling adverts on social media,' he said. 'In-game gambling and loot boxes are a new phenomenon and so require new answers. The world has changed since 2005 when the gambling sector was deregulated and so, sadly, has gambling.

'Therefore, government, local authorities, schools, the private and the charitable sector need to study these findings carefully and put in place preventative measures to safeguard young people.'

21 November 2018

www.theguardian.com

Gambling websites must stop appealing to children, regulators warn

Games featuring brightly coloured cartoon characters among those highlighted as 'unacceptable'.

By Chris Baynes

Gambling websites have been ordered to immediately remove 'unacceptable' adverts likely to appeal to children.

Regulators have jointly written to operators urging them to advertise responsibly and threatening them with sanctions if they fail to comply.

The highlighted games with names such as *Fluffy Favourites* and *Pirate Princess*, which featured brightly coloured cartoon characters, as examples likely to lure children into gambling.

The letter was sent to more than 450 operators by the Gambling Commission, the Advertising Standards Authority, the Committee of Advertising Practice (CAP) and the Remote Gambling Association said.

Under-18s and other vulnerable people should be protected from exploitation, the regulators stressed.

The letter said: 'We are writing to advise you to amend or remove immediately any ads on your website or in third-party media that are likely to appeal particularly to people aged 17 or younger… and generally available to view.

'This relates particularly to freely accessible ads for play-for-free and play-for-money games and includes all graphics and images displayed on a website or in third-party media.

'The use of particular colours, cartoons and comic book images, animals, child and youth-orientated references and names of games such as *Piggy Payout*, *Fluffy Favourites*, *Pirate Princess* and *Jack and the Beanstalk* are likely, alone or in combination, to enhance appeal to under-18s.'

It added: 'You must immediately amend or remove any freely accessible ads on your website or in third-party media space that are likely to appeal particularly to under-18s.'

The letter warned of possible sanctions should sites fail to comply with the CAP code, which requires marketing communications for gambling to be socially responsible.

About 450,000 children gamble on a weekly basis, research by the Gambling Commission found last year. About 9,000 of those were described as 'problem gamblers'.

The Local Government Association (LGA) backed the crackdown, saying councils had previously asked for greater restrictions.

Councillor Simon Blackburn, chairman of the LGA's Safer and Stronger Communities Board, said: 'Problem gambling is a major concern for councils, which can cause greater personal harm.

'It can lead to spiralling debt, deteriorating mental health and wellbeing, and a toll on society – and taxpayers – through crime and disorder, family breakdown and homelessness.

'It is vital our children and young people are kept safe and protected from the problems gambling can cause.'

22 October 2017

Matt Zarb-Cousin: blanket advertising is turning our children into gambling addicts

Hearing from the Gambling Commission that 61,000 11–16-year-olds in Britain have a gambling addiction, or are at risk of developing one, should shock us – but it shouldn't surprise us. Britain is the only country in the world that lets children gamble on low-stake machines at seaside amusement arcades.

But ten years since New Labour's disastrous Gambling Act came into force, which ushered in an era of promoting gambling as a 'legitimate entertainment activity', both the advances in technology and the bizarre pre-watershed exemption for gambling ads during live sporting events has given rise to a wholesale conditioning of children to associate betting with every aspect of life. Enshrined in the Gambling Act, one of three licensing objectives is to prevent harm to the young and the vulnerable, which the Gambling Commission is supposed to enforce.

It could not be any clearer now that it is failing to uphold what must be considered the most basic tenet of the law. Gambling has a similar effect on the brain to cocaine addiction, yet more than one in ten 11–16-year-old children take part in 'skins' betting – in which online games allow players to buy and sell virtual items with a real monetary value – or they've played casino games on Facebook or smartphone apps.

Bombarded with advertising

After a decade of bombarding children with gambling adverts – 80% have seen them on TV and 70% through social

media – 370,000 of 11–16-year-olds now gamble, starting at an average age of just 12.

This is storing up problems for the future. Young people are more likely to get addicted as the brain doesn't fully develop, and is not able to properly regulate risk, until a person is into their 20s. Which is why two in five young people gamble not as 'legitimate entertainment' but to make money.

Even though preventing under 18s from gambling appears to be beyond the scope of the current regulator, there's a strong argument for raising the age at which it's legally permitted to 21.

Most 18–21-year-olds are either in full-time education, training or insecure work. Yet if you walk around a Fresher's Fair on any university campus, there are gambling companies promoting themselves to young people.

A study by the Victorian Responsible Gambling Foundation found that three-quarters of children as young as eight could correctly recall a sports betting brand, the high frequency of marketing led them to believe betting was a part of sport, and 'cash back' offers contributed to a perception that you could not lose from gambling.

Today's tobacco ads

The UK Government is currently reviewing the maximum stake on the bookies' £100-a-spin Fixed Odds Betting Terminals, and a reduction to £2 a spin is long overdue. But they look set to duck a crackdown on advertising, favouring an industry-funded 'responsible gambling' ad campaign instead, costing around £5 million. Hardly a counterweight to the £360 million a year the industry spends on marketing. But it'll be no surprise if the status quo is maintained when gambling falls under the remit of the Department for Culture, Media and Sport. It's likely the TV companies have been lobbying that government department as much as the betting industry to prevent any advertising restrictions, so dependent are they on the revenue those ads brings in. But it's a sign of a broken economy when gambling companies are the monoliths they've become. Where they sponsor half of Premier League football teams, and create a culture where sports betting and casino games – often operated by tax-avoiding companies based offshore – are so normalised that children are getting addicted to them. One day we'll look back on this era of relentless gambling advertising in the same way we recount tobacco ads – asking ourselves, 'what the hell were we thinking?' Hopefully that day is in the not-too-distant future.

12 December 2017

Skin gambling: teenage Britain's secret habit

An extract from a report by Parent Zone: The experts in digital family life

What is skin gambling?

A brief history of skins

Skins are virtual items that can be won or purchased within certain video games to decorate and customise weapons. They rarely affect gameplay and are mainly aesthetic but, due to their popularity, a marketplace has developed for the trading of skins.

Skins were popularised in the 2012 video game *Counter Strike: Global Offensive (CS:GO)*, owned by the US-based Valve Corporation. Valve also developed the Steam platform, which lets players buy, sell or trade their personal skin collections for real or virtual currency.

As a result, individual skins have developed unique values, based on market demand. In this process, skins have themselves become a virtual online currency.

The rise of skin gambling

As the popularity of *CS:GO* grew as an esport – a form of competitive gaming played and watched by millions of fans worldwide – interest grew in betting on major esports matches. By 2015, third-party sites, which had been set up to support the trading of skins, began to offer users the chance to bet on live esports matches. In 2016, sites began to offer additional jackpot options for skin betting, including games like roulette and coin tosses. These casino games are high frequency and gamblers can place a new bet as regularly as every 30 seconds.

While you cannot withdraw money from Steam or the third-party gambling sites, additional sites emerged, which allowed users to exchange skins for cash – or, in essence, cash in their chips.

These casino-style sites grew in popularity to the point now where one industry expert predicted the total global value of skins gambled in 2018 would reach over £10 billion.[1]

Unlicensed and unregulated

Valve's Steam Market facilitates these betting sites, because it operates an application programming interface (API), meaning outside developers have access to its programming code. This allows players to log in to their Steam accounts from third-party websites and access their skins.

Like Steam, few third-party gambling sites use age verification, and do not operate under any gambling licensing or regulatory bodies. This means anyone with a Steam account can enter third-party sites and gamble. Steam, in response, has issued a cease and desist lawsuit to 21 unaffiliated sites, yet this only had partial success and many new sites continue to emerge.

1. *https://www.linkedin.com/pulse/skin-gambling-crackdown-controversies-likely-shave-billions-grove/*

Loot boxes and mystery chests

Skin gambling can come in other forms, such as 'loot boxes' and 'mystery chests'. In these, players can spend real money to buy hidden items, usually hoping to get a rare or valuable skin. The risk is getting one worth less than the price paid for the box, or a duplicate of what they already own. Often, the odds of success in these boxes are not disclosed, so young people can be drawn into gambling on what they might get, without knowing their true odds of success, or how the results are regulated.

'I've got a friend who tried one of the websites. He has a huge collection of skins for a game… £1,000 worth. He put £1 on it just to try it out and he wanted to do a bit more cos he lost and wanted to get it back. He lost again and wanted to get his £10 back. He ended up winning £750, but he's really addicted to it. He's 15.'

Boy, 14

Methodology

Parent Zone set out to understand the scale of skin gambling by UK children, and to find out how they are doing it.

We commissioned an Ipsos MORI survey* with 1,001 children aged 13 to 18 to find out what they know about skin gambling. The survey was conducted with parental permission.

We additionally visited six UK secondary schools between 6 March 2018 and 7 June 2018, speaking confidentially to mixed groups of boys and girls, aged 12 to 16. We asked them to discuss what they knew about skin gambling, Steam, third-party gambling sites and the culture that surrounds them. All names have been omitted to protect identity.

In order to understand the skin gambling process, we conducted an investigation using the identity of a 14-year-old. Using the child's personal details, including genuine name, address and account information, we attempted to gamble skins in the way described to us by the children we met. The investigation was undertaken with full parental permission and cooperation.

* The research was carried out by Ipsos MORI on behalf of Parent Zone. It surveyed a nationally representative quota sample of 1,001 children in the United Kingdom aged 13-18 using an online survey between 25 May and 4 June 2018. Data have been weighted by age, gender, region to the known offline population profile.

How many UK children are skin gambling?

27% of children aged 13–18 have heard of skin gambling.

10% have gambled skins in some form.

29% think it is a 'very big' or 'fairly big' problem.

It is perhaps no surprise to know that 90% of 13–18-year-olds in the UK play games online. It is, however, a surprise to know that nearly a third of these children have heard of skin gambling (30%) – especially to the many adults who are neither aware of it, nor know how widespread skin gambling has become in little over two years.

When Parent Zone ran focus groups at schools across the UK, we found four of the six groups were aware of skin gambling, and those that were had a sophisticated understanding of the process. They all understood that it is gambling, although in a different form to the types you might find in familiar high-street bookmakers or popular online gambling platforms. Most agreed that while skins are used as a virtual currency, the potential to win or lose actual money was very real.

Our survey confirmed it is widespread, with 10% of children across the UK aged 13–18 revealing they have gambled skins in some form. This percentage amounts to approximately 448,744 children in the UK aged 13–18.[2]

'[A skin] is basically just money cos… you can buy them with real money and you can sell them for real money, it's just like kind of a… currency.'

Boy, 13

'What people do is they put certain items up for sale and people can buy them for real money, so that means certain skins have a certain value associated with them… The gambling site uses this monetary value of skins as currency on their websites.'

Boy, 15

'There's websites that gamble skins… You put them on these websites and then there's a chance to get a better skin or a worse skin, and you can lose loads of money on there. That's basically just gambling, they just cover it up… cos you use the skins instead of currency.'

Boy, 13

2. Office for National Statistics Population Overview, February 2016.

Of all those children who have heard of skin gambling…

36% have gambled skins

While over one in three of those children who have heard of skin gambling have tried it for themselves, our focus group responses to skin gambling were neither overly positive or negative.

This is in contrast to some of the videos you can find on YouTube or Twitch, which feature high-value gambling wins. Videos with titles such as 'CRAZY 1% CHANCE $4,000 WIN!!' (1.5m views), 'MOE WINS $84,000! CS:GO SKIN GAMBLING!' (349k views) and 'CS:GO Gambling – ACCIDENTAL 56,000$ WIN!' (259k views) offer a distorted view of skin gambling that is unlikely to be replicated.

Indeed, few of our focus group participants had enjoyed a particularly rewarding experience while some had lost a high value of skins. One boy, 13, told us how he had traded to earn £2,000-worth of skins, only to lose most of them gambling on third-party websites.

'I sold my whole skin collection to gamble on the website but didn't make money… I lost all my skins and left with worse skins.'

Boy, 13

'You think you can do what they [YouTubers] do, pretty much all of my YouTube time is gaming – watch them and then be like, I can try that.'

Boy, 13

'I had a friend who skin gambled. He stopped a long time ago. He lost a lot of money.'

Boy, 15

It's not just a boy thing...

While our research confirmed that boys are clearly the more engaged when it comes to gaming, one in five of all the children we surveyed that have skin gambled were female. While this cross-segment is too small to make an accurate estimate on a national level, the figure shows that it is not just an issue affecting boys.

How do they pay for it?

Skins can be won in games, such as *CS:GO* or *League of Legends*, obtained via the purchase of an in-game mystery box, traded for in the Steam marketplace, or bought from other users.

Most of the children we surveyed who had skin gambled had used real money to do so, mainly using pocket or gift money from parents and family.

However, as our focus groups revealed, what their parents knew they were doing with the money could vary dramatically.

'[My parents] know about it… As long as it's coming from my account and it's legal, my mum and dad don't particularly mind.'

Boy, 15

'I've got my own bank account so whatever money is in there I don't really ask – I just spend it. There's loads of £2/£3 micro-transactions that I do all the time, that can sum up to a lot, but they don't really know about that. They know that I'm spending it, just they don't know what on.'

Boy, 13

'People playing online games doing this might just think its harmless fun when really they have a problem and cannot see it for themselves.'

Boy, 14

46% of children across the UK aged 13–17 say they are able to access 18+ websites if they want.

Age verification technology varies between different websites which offer skin gambling services. This might explain why nearly half of the children we surveyed told us that they could bypass age restrictions on over-18s websites. Regardless of what children may have to do to access services designed for over-18s – from accepting a site's user agreement to faking age-verification checks – it is clear children believe they can access sites not intended for their use.

Britain's youngest Euromillions winner drops plans to sue lottery bosses for 'ruining her life'

Jane Park says her newly accumulated wealth made her life 'ten times worse'.

By Mary Oppenheim

Britain's youngest Euromillions winner has dropped her plans to take legal action against lottery bosses for 'ruining her life'. Jane Park, who won £1 million at the age of 17, threatened to sue bosses for negligence and argued someone of her age should not have been allowed to win so much money. Ms Park, now 21, argued 18 should be the minimum age to win.

The teenage millionaire, from Edinburgh, has now backtracked over plans to take legal action. Ms Park said she had already achieved her goal of raising awareness for the age limit to be raised.

After being asked on *Loose Women* on Wednesday, whether she planned to sue, Ms Park said: 'No. What I said was me phoning up the lottery and saying, "I think 16 is too young, you should up the age to 18", they were never going to be like, "Jane that's great advice, we'll up our age"

'So what I did was, I'd only spoke to a lawyer, I was just wanting to seek legal advice just to get my point across, get it out there.'

'But because it has gone so far already, I won't even have to go any further, I feel like I have been listened to now and people are actually listening to the difficulties.'

Before winning the lottery, Ms Park, who now owns two properties, worked as an admin temp for £8 an hour and lived in a small flat with her mum in Edinburgh.

Appearing on BBC's *Victoria Derbyshire Show* on Thursday, Ms Park said winning the lottery had been a very stressful experience at times.

'I never realised I would've felt at times like I'd ruined my life when I was 17. Now I get days when I get these feelings and I think I wish I'd never even won it,' she said.

'It was a ridiculous amount to have at such a young age with no guidance... I wish I didn't have the stress and pressure at such a young age.'

Ms Park said it was difficult to constantly feel obliged to give those close to you money when they are struggling. Despite being unhappy at times, she said she did not want to give her hefty windfall away because she wanted to have children in the future and be able to provide for both them and her wider family.

This echoes her comments over the weekend where she said she had become tired of consumption as it failed to offer long-term genuine happiness or satisfaction. She said winning the lottery had made her life 'ten times worse' and it sometimes felt like it had 'ruined' her life altogether.

Despite the fact that Camelot, which runs EuroMillions in the UK, appointed an adviser to help Ms Park deal with her newly accumulated wealth, she told the *Sunday People* it was family advice that helped her keep tabs on her spending.

'People look at me and think,"I wish I had her lifestyle, I wish I had her money." But they don't realise the extent of my stress. I have material things but apart from that my life is empty. What is my purpose in life?'

A spokesperson for Camelot told *The Independent*: 'Camelot takes its duty of care to winners very seriously and all major winners are offered support and advice for as long as they wish. That support is tailored to each winner's situation and circumstances – and for younger winners, their age will obviously be an important factor in the advice and support offered.

'Following her win, Jane received extensive support from Camelot,' it continued. 'A dedicated winners' adviser visited Jane at home to pay out her prize, arrange private banking and support her through the publicity when she chose to share news of her win. An independent financial and legal panel was set up shortly after her win and we put Jane in touch with another winner who won at the same age, to share their experience and help Jane adjust to the win.

'We keep in contact with all major winners for as long as they wish and have been in touch with Jane from time to time since her win to offer ongoing support. Of course, it is always up to the winners themselves as to whether they want to take us up on that ongoing support and advice – but the door is always open and we will continue to support Jane in any way we can if that is what she decides she wants.'

Camelot said the minimum age limit to play the lottery was an issue for Parliament to deal with rather than themselves.

'Anyone over the age of 16 can play the lottery, and therefore win a prize,' they said in a statement. 'Camelot doesn't set the age limit to play – this was agreed at the launch of the National Lottery back in 1994 and so any questions about the legal age to play would be a matter for Parliament.'

While most who play the lottery fantasise about the moment of hearing their lucky numbers called out and winning the jackpot, the reality of winning can be very different. There are a number of stories of lottery winners who have struggled to get used to becoming wealthy overnight and no longer working.

16 February 2017

Belgium is right to class video game loot boxes as child gambling

Belgium's Gaming Commission has decided that 'loot box' mechanics in three popular video games encourage children to gamble. The games industry doesn't need them.

By Keza MacDonald

In April, the Belgian minister of justice, Koen Geens, announced the result of an investigation that the country's Gaming Commission conducted into video game 'loot boxes', a mechanic that lets players pay real money for a chance at winning virtual items. It found that three popular games – *Overwatch*, *Counter-Strike: Global Offensive* and *Fifa 18* – were in violation of gambling legislation. This is a significant finding, because controversy over loot boxes has been raging for at least six months: are they actually a form of gambling? Worse, are they a form of gambling that is particularly appealing to children?

Belgium's Gaming Commission has decided that, yes, they are, and the publishers in question should remove loot boxes from their games or face fines. (EA and Blizzard, publishers of two of the games in question, did not respond to requests for comment on how they plan to comply; a Valve spokesperson said that the company is 'happy to engage with the Belgian Gambling Commission and answer any questions they may have.') There might be no financial incentive to buying loot boxes – you never win any

money – but they are still a game of chance. 'A dialogue with the sector is necessary,' said Geens: 'It is often children who come into contact with such systems and we can not allow that.'

Often when governments get involved with trying to legislate over video games – as President Trump threatened to do after the Florida school shooting in February – it comes from a place of moral panic, and a lack of understanding of games themselves. A spurious causal link is drawn between video games and violence, or truancy, or mental health problems in young people. Despite decades of research showing no correlation between violent games and violent behaviour, and despite the fact games are played and enjoyed by hundreds of millions of people without social collapse.

In the case of loot boxes, though, the Belgian Government is spot on. There are better ways to make money than applying gambling principles to video games that ought to be harmless fun.

Loot boxes exist because video-game development on a large scale is an increasingly expensive business. The development costs of blockbuster-style games have increased tenfold in ten years, according to data compiled by industry veteran Raph Koster, with budgets now running into hundreds of millions of dollars. Players, however, are reluctant to accept price increases; a newly released game still costs £50–£60, pretty much the same as it did 15 years ago. Pricing hasn't even kept up with inflation.

To address the shortfall, video game publishers have devised various ways of enabling players to spend extra money. For instance, DLC (downloadable content) offers virtual cosmetic items to customise a character, new story chapters to play through, or extra maps to battle upon – all optional. It has also become customary to offer a 'season pass' to players – pay an extra £10 to £30 or so, and you'll have access to all the extra content

that's released for a game over time. Online modes keep people playing for months or years rather than weeks, and players can pay to customise a character or buy a new car or in-game apartment – usually with either real money, or in-game money that takes time to earn.

Loot boxes, however, are a fairly new invention – one that crossed over from free-to-play smartphone games, which have traditionally been less scrupulous about wheedling money out of players (and, perhaps consequently, been more successful at doing so). With a loot box, you pay for a chance to obtain a virtual item – usually with real money. It's a slot-machine-style system where, although you're guaranteed to get something on every spin, the chance of getting what you actually want is vastly reduced.

This works on the same part of the brain as any game of chance; the dopamine hit is enjoyable, but potentially addictive, and hard to resist. Players quite regularly spend hundreds on loot boxes – just ask players of *Fifa Ultimate Team*, who can buy Team Packs in the hope of unlocking a coveted player.

The Belgian report found several issues with loot boxes: the rewards are uncertain, causing an emotional reaction; players can be misled into believing they are buying an advantage; popular YouTubers and other celebrities promote them; the actual chance of receiving particular items is often hidden from the player. The exposure of these chance mechanics to children was a particular concern.

'Mixing games and gambling, especially at a young age, is dangerous for mental health,' said Geens. 'We must ensure that children and adults are not presented with games of chance when they are looking for fun in a video game.'

Gamers everywhere would welcome the removal of these insidious inventions. There is nothing worse than feeling forced to spend money to keep up in a video game, especially when spending money doesn't even guarantee you the item that you want. Adults might find it easy to resist the appeal of new gun skins in *Counter-Strike*, or outfits for *Overwatch* characters, but for the teens who predominantly play these games, that perspective may be lacking.

One need only look to *Fortnite*, one of the most popular games in the world right now, to see things done right: in *Fortnite* you can pay about £8 for a Battle Pass every few months, which unlocks fun new challenges and lets you earn all the new stuff you could want, just by playing.

Games are getting more and more expensive to make, but the video games industry should not need to employ the tricks of the gambling industry to plug the gap. If the Belgian Government's decision leads to a Europe-wide ruling on loot boxes, hopefully publishers will be forced to come up with better ways to monetise their games – and players might have to get comfortable with the idea of paying more for them in the first place.

26 April 2018

Video games that offer random rewards to children linked with problem gambling, study finds

By Mike Wright

Children who play computer games that offer randomised rewards could be more likely to become problem gamblers in adulthood, the first study to show a link has found.

A study by the universities of York and York St John found adult gamers with a history of problem gambling spent more on paid-for features in video games, known as loot boxes, which dispense random items such as in-game weapons or characters.

Researchers said the findings, which came from surveys of more than 7,400 gamers, established a 'significant relationship' between problem gambling and loot boxes.

They also warned that the features, used in popular titles such as *Rocket League* and *Overwatch*, 'may well be acting as a gateway to problem gambling'.

Loot boxes appear in games rated appropriate for three-year-olds and above and it is estimated that $30 billion (£23 billion) has been spent on them in 2018.

One of the authors of the study, Paul Cairns, from the University of York, said: '[The games industry has said] it's not gambling, it doesn't look like gambling, it's different.

'But what we are saying is, okay, whatever you can define gambling as, the behaviours are overlapping with problem gambling behaviours and that's an issue.'

In the study, researchers asked gamers how much they spent on loot boxes on a monthly basis and then assessed them against the Problem Gambling Severity Index.

The study found: 'The more severe that participants' problem gambling was, the more money they spent on loot boxes.'

Mr Cairns added: 'What we don't know is how children are responding to this. If adults are having this link, what else may be happening with children? As a parent I would be very concerned.'

Loot boxes are currently not classed as gambling by the Gambling Commission as their prizes are deemed to have no monetary value.

Following the study, Prof. Mark Griffiths, of Nottingham Trent University and a leading expert on addiction, called on the Gambling Commission to alter its interpretation of the Gambling Act 2005 to include loot boxes.

He said: 'To me loot boxes are gambling, they are akin to a lottery. Some people argue it's not gambling if you always win something, but if the item you win is far less than the money you paid for, then for me that's not really a win.

'The Gambling Commission will admit that loot boxes are gambling-like – I think most people would say they are gambling-like – even if they are not by their own definitions a form of gambling. I have argued that it is a form of gambling.

Regulators around the world are starting to examine the issue of loot boxes and earlier this year Belgium's gambling commission ruled they were a form of gambling.

The UK commission said it is currently investigating areas where it is concerned about increasingly 'blurred lines' between video games and gambling.

A spokeman said: 'The Gambling Commission is aware of the study and welcomes academic research in this area given the concerns that exist. This is why we have joined forces with other regulators to call on video games companies to address the clear public concern around the risks gambling and some video games can pose to children.'

Following the study, The Association for UK Interactive Entertainment (UKie), which represents the games industry, said loot boxes were an optional feature in games.

Dr Jo Twist OBE, CEO of Ukie said: 'Loot boxes and the purchasing of in-game items more generally are always optional and are covered by and fully compliant with existing relevant UK regulations and do not constitute gambling in UK law.

'Games businesses do not allow, facilitate, or condone the conversion of virtual currencies or other in-game items into money or the use of them within unlicensed third-party gambling sites, so called "skin betting/gambling". The industry works with regulators to stop unlicensed sites from operating.'

7 December 2017

YouTubers criticised for promoting 'loot box' gambling games to young children

By Natasha Bernal

Popular YouTubers have come under fire for promoting controversial games linked to gambling to young viewers.

Jake Paul and Brian 'RiceGum' Lee, who have 28.5 million subscribers between them, were among those criticised for posting sponsored videos showing them spending money on 'loot boxes'.

Loot boxes, which appear in video games, prompt players to spend money in exchange for random in-game purchases.

In new promotional videos, both Jake Paul and Brian 'RiceGum' Lee clicked on online mystery treasure chests and revealed they had won real-life objects including Apple AirPods and trainers worth $1,000.

MysteryBrand, the company behind the promotional videos, offers a real-life version of these boxes that can cost between $3.99 (£3.16) and $1,300 (£1,028) apiece.

Each box contains a range of possible pre-selected items but a user has no idea what they will get until they have paid.

MysteryBrand is understood to have paid $100,000 for the videos, which were lambasted by the duo's viewers as well as YouTubers Ethan Klein, Kavos and PewDiePie.

PewDiePie, whose real name is Felix Kjellberg, released a video where he called the videos 'an oopsie'.

He said: 'They both have considerably young fans, and promoting a gambling website in general just seems like a bad idea for these people to do. And they obviously don't care.'

On Twitter, Ethan Klein said: 'Jake Paul and RiceGum are running a nice little gambling scam to usher in the new year.'

The UK's Gambling Commission told *The Telegraph* that it would assess the website that commissioned the videos and 'take appropriate action'.

RiceGum defended himself in a video posted on Thursday, saying 'I don't even think it's a big deal.'

He said: 'It's a common thing when YouTubers work with brands and sponsored videos.'

RiceGum also complained that another YouTube accounts had done similar videos in the past without any backlash.

He said: 'I'm not going to sit here and bring up everyone who did the same deal as me, I'm just trying to say this mystery box thing has been on the internet for like, three or four months from other creators but as soon as I do it, it's a problem.

'I do feel bad, I mean I am defending myself, but I do know I'm somewhat in the wrong. It's true, I'm an a------le but the damage has been done, you guys have seen a money hungry side of me and there is nothing I can really do but say sorry.'

One YouTube user commenting on the Jake Paul video said: 'It's certainly disturbing to see you promoting gambling to your underage audience. That website is beyond sketchy by the way.'

The Gambling Commission has previously said that loot boxes 'blur the lines' between video games and gambling and pledged to 'thoroughly analyse' how loot boxes are designed to ensure they comply with gambling laws.

Loot boxes are worth a reported $30 billion and are set to exceed $50 billion by 2022, according to data from Juniper Research.

YouTube has not banned advertising for gambling, but does not allow links to online gambling casinos

A YouTube spokesman said: 'YouTube believes that creators should be transparent with their audiences if their content includes paid promotion of any kind. Our policies make it clear that YouTube creators are responsible for ensuring their content complies with local laws, regulations and YouTube Community Guidelines.

'If content is found to violate these policies, we take action to ensure the integrity of our platform, which can include removing content.'

4 January 2019

More than just financial loss, the social impact of gambling cannot be underestimated

THE CONVERSATION

An article from **The Conversation.**

By Crystal Fulton, Associate Professor of Information & Communication Studies, University College Dublin

The UK Government is mulling a review of the regulations on fixed odds betting terminals commonly found in pubs and betting shops, in order to reduce the risk of problem gambling developing.

Based on a report from the UK Department for Digital, Culture, Media and Sport, this would see the maximum stake gamblers can bet on the machines reduced from £300 a minute to between £2 and £50.

Given that the Gambling Commission, the industry regulator, found 43% of people who use the machines are either problem or at-risk gamblers, some such as opposition Labour MP Tom Watson, have described this as 'a squandered opportunity'. Critics believe the proposals don't go far enough to protect people from fixed odds betting terminals, sometimes described as 'the crack cocaine of gambling' due to their addictive nature.

Harmful gambling can have crippling financial and social effects on the gambler, their friends and family. In the first national study of the social impact of harmful gambling in Ireland, we examined how it affected recovering gamblers, their families and friends. We also heard stories from counsellors and those who provide services to help gamblers. Talking to people from all walks of life, from different age groups and different economic backgrounds, we found that a common theme was the devastating social effects gambling had on people's lives.

In particular, we learned that gamblers were often exposed to gambling at an early age, for example by collecting betting proceeds for a family member, or watching adults place bets. This then led them to participate in gambling before the legal age of 18.

Gamblers reported gambling in secret, isolating themselves from family and friends to feed their addiction. As relationships deteriorated, the gambler's behaviour would only be discovered when they were no longer able to maintain a double life, such as failing to intercept unpaid bills that had been part of trying to maintain a facade of normality. The availability of technologies, such as smartphones, means that it's possible to conceal a secret gambling habit for years, before financial and emotional crises reach breaking point.

For young people, such technology exacerbates the potential harm of gambling. The participants in our studies frequently spoke of their concern for young people and their risk of addiction due to the availability of gambling apps and websites easily accessible from their smartphones. And while there is supposedly agreement not to offer fixed odds betting terminals in Ireland, some gamblers reported that they had got themselves into trouble using them.

Gambling as a public health issue

The social harms that stem from addictive gambling are not only for the gambler. For example, the wives of gamblers in our study reported how they could sense there was a problem, but believed they were struggling with marital issues, rather than the fallout from gambling addiction. Parents and children of gamblers reported that they could no longer trust the gambler, that they could no longer leave money unattended, and that the gambler had become someone they did not recognise or understand.

In Ireland, the legislation around regulating gambling is outdated. The regulations that might mitigate harms for the individual and for society have not been introduced, and – with support from the Irish Research Council and Ireland's Department of Social Protection and Department of Justice and Equality – our research sought to provide the evidence base to help draw up the necessary social policies.

The Government indicated its intention to move forward with legislation in early 2017, and my research and its follow-up study should inform politicians how to address the social harms of gambling – the costs of which the Institute of Public Health in Ireland has estimated to be greater than government revenue from gambling taxes.

Listen to what gamblers say they need

The participants interviewed said there is a need for open discussion about gambling and the risk it can pose to individuals and their families. Gambling addiction carries with it significant social stigma, shame and isolation – talking openly about its effects can change how we approach this issue.

Interviewees suggested a variety of measures government could take, including regulations that would protect the most vulnerable to gambling addiction, and particularly in regulating how technology now enables secretive gambling. They also identified the need for support that would help prevent and address the harmful effects of gambling addiction.

While there are addiction treatment centres around the country which include services to address harmful gambling, there is little help for those affected by a partner's or family member's gambling. The RISE Foundation is a notable exception, providing treatment for the families of those affected by a variety of addictions. But it is based in Dublin only, and family members may no longer have the financial resources to access treatment and support there.

There is an urgent need for a unified, transparent approach to tackling gambling's harms in Ireland – a national strategy that encompasses public and private sector organisations, similar to those that target alcohol and drug addiction. The UK has the Gambling Commission and NHS support and advice; Ireland has nothing comparable.

Despite the lack of progress from government on the issue there have been benefits to this research: uncovering the extent of gambling's social harms has helped to get people talking about gambling. For example, in September 2017 the European United Left–Nordic Green Left European Parliamentary Group sponsored a one-day conference in Dublin to direct the spotlight on the subject and emphasise the need for updated legislation.

Within the Republic, Problem Gambling Ireland recently opened its doors to lobby against the spread of harmful gambling and to provide referral services to those affected by gambling. These may seem like small steps, but it is small steps that lead the charge for change.

1 November 2017

Government to slash maximum stake on fixed-odds betting terminals to £2 in bid to tackle problem gambling

Controversial machines currently allow users to bet up to £100 every 20 seconds on virtual casino games and horse racing.

By Tom Barnes

The maximum stake on fixed-odds betting terminals (FOBT) will be cut from £100 to £2, the Government has announced.

The move follows lengthy consultations over the machines, dubbed the 'crack cocaine of gambling' by critics due to their potentially addictive nature.

Bookmakers have previously claimed moves to slash the maximum stake on FOBTs would lead to the loss of thousands of jobs in the industry.

The Government said the new measures would cut the potential for gamblers to rack up huge losses and reduce harm inflicted as a result on the wider community.

'Problem gambling can devastate individuals' lives, families and communities,' said sports minister Tracey Crouch, announcing the move on Thursday.

'It is right that we take decisive action now to ensure a responsible gambling industry that protects the most vulnerable in our society.

'By reducing FOBT stakes to £2 we can help stop extreme losses by those who can least afford it.

'While we want a healthy gambling industry that contributes to the economy, we also need one that does all it can to protect players.'

FOBTs currently allow users to bet between £1 and £100 every 20 seconds on casino games such as virtual roulette, or simulated horse and greyhound races.

The British public loses around £1.8 billion each year betting on the machines, according to figures released by the Gambling Commission.

Bookmaker William Hill warned the decision to limit the maximum stake on FOBTs could see around 900 of its shops become loss-making, adding a 'proportion' risked closure.

'The Government has handed us a tough challenge today and it will take some time for the full impact to be understood, for our business, the wider high street and key

partners like horse racing,' said William Hill chief executive Philip Bowcock.

'We will continue to evolve our retail business in order to adapt to this change and we will support our colleagues as best we can.

'Despite the challenges presented by this decision, our teams will compete hard and offer great service to William Hill customers.'

Gambling giant Paddy Power Betfair said it welcomed the move to help improve the sector's image, but warned it could hit its gaming revenues by between £35 million and £46 million.

'We have previously highlighted our concern that the wider gambling industry has suffered reputational damage as a result of the widespread unease over stake limits on gaming machines,' said Peter Jackson, the firm's chief executive.

'We welcome, therefore, the significant intervention by the Government today, and believe this is a positive development for the long-term sustainability of the industry.'

Campaign group Fairer Gambling said the Government's decision to cut maximum FOBT stakes to £2 was 'the right one'.

'The evidence shows this policy will reduce harm for those experiencing it, and eliminate the most addictive roulette content, significantly reducing problem gambling associated with FOBTs,' a spokesman added.

Labour's shadow culture secretary Tom Watson hailed the announcement as the end of a 'reign of destruction and misery' caused by FOBTs, but warned new limits would not solve wider issues surrounding gambling addiction.

'It is a victory for cross-party campaigners who have worked tirelessly for this day over many years,' he said.

'This won't be a silver bullet for the wider epidemic of problem gambling in the UK but it will go a long way to solving what has been a particular evil for too long.

'It's not often that the opposition congratulates a government minister, but Tracey Crouch has made the right decision today.'

17 May 2017

Sports minister resigns over delay to gambling curb

By Rob Davies

Sports minister Tracey Crouch has resigned in protest at the Government's 'unjustifiable' refusal to speed up plans to curb controversial fixed-odds betting terminals (FOBTs).

Crouch, who launched the review that concluded that FOBT stakes should be slashed from £100 to £2, quit after the chancellor revealed in this week's budget that the change would not take effect until October next year. The Conservative MP had lobbied hard for the cut to be implemented as soon as possible, in April 2019.

In a letter to the prime minister, Crouch said the stake cut was being delayed 'due to commitments made by others to those with registered interests'.

The comment is thought to be a reference to lobbying efforts by MPs with ties to the betting industry to postpone the cut in stakes.

'From the time of the announcement to reduce stakes and its implementation, £1.6 billion will be lost on these machines, a significant amount of which will be in our most deprived areas, including my own constituency,' Crouch wrote. "In addition, two people will tragically take their lives every day

due to gambling-related problems and for that reason as much as any other I believe this delay is unjustifiable.'

She added that 'ministers must adhere to collective responsibility and cannot disagree with policy, let alone when it's policy made against your wishes relating to your own portfolio'.

In her response, Theresa May contradicted Crouch, saying there had been 'no delay'.

She wrote that the Government had 'listened to those who wanted it to come into effect earlier than April 2020 and have agreed that changes should be in place within the year – by October 2019'.

Crouch is understood to have clashed with Jeremy Wright, the minister for the Department for Digital, Culture, Media & Sport (DCMS), over the delay, with the sports minister insisting that April 2019 was a red line for her.

Prior to this week's announcement, she had repeatedly said on the record that the step would be put before MPs before next week's parliamentary recess and introduced by next April. That raised the possibility the minister had

either been cut out of the decision or overruled on it. The six-month postponement, which will allow bookmakers to collect an extra £900 million from the machines, has also sparked outcry among campaigners and MPs.

Wright defended the delay in parliament on Thursday in the face of fierce criticism from both sides of the house, including from the former Tory leader, Iain Duncan Smith. Duncan Smith later invited the chief secretary to the Treasury, Liz Truss, to consider bringing forward the cut in the House of Commons on Thursday evening, amid speculation that Crouch's threat to resign had forced the government into a Uturn. Truss said: 'I don't believe it's an issue for the finance bill, but I'm happy to discuss with my honourable friend about what more we can do.'

Crouch is now likely to add her name to a planned amendment to the finance bill, the act that implements the budget. Duncan Smith and Labour MP Carolyn Harris are expected to lay the amendment, which is believed to have the support of about 35 Tory rebels, leaving the Government facing the prospect of a bruising defeat.

The Archbishop of Canterbury praised her stance over FOBTs on Thursday night. Justin Welby tweeted that Crouch was 'principled and courageous … May God bless her commitment to doing right'. People close to Crouch said her resolve had been hardened by meetings with the parents of children who took their own lives after becoming addicted to gambling through FOBTs.

In a letter to Philip Hammond, some of the parents who Crouch met told the chancellor he would be 'morally bankrupt' if he allowed bookies to maintain FOBTs at £100 a spin until October.

The Gambling With Lives group told Hammond that "FOBTs were an instrumental factor in our children's deaths.' Every month the reduced stake implementation is delayed sees tens of thousands more young people becoming addicted, and dozens of gambling-related suicides.

'The chancellor would be morally bankrupt should he continue to side with the bookmakers and allow them to profit at the expense of young people's lives. How many more lives need to be lost before the Government finally acts and implements the reduced FOBT stake?'

Labour's deputy leader and shadow DCMS minister Tom Watson said: 'Tracey Crouch has taken a courageous and principled decision to resign from the Government over Jeremy Wright's decision to delay cutting the maximum stake on FOBTs. "She poured her heart and soul into a significant review of these destructive machines, faced down a systematic lobbying attempt by the gambling industry, and took the right decision for those suffering from problem gambling, their families and communities.

'The new secretary of state has threatened all of this good work. He has prioritised corporate interests over victims, profits over public health and greed over good. He should be thoroughly ashamed.' Speaking in the House of Commons earlier, Wright said the stake cut had not been delayed but had in fact been brought forward from an earlier planned date of April 2020. He said the gambling industry needed time to prepare for the economic impact of the changes.

FOBTs are worth about £1.8 billionn a year to bookmakers, who have warned of shop closures and thousands of a job losses as a result of stakes being cut to £2. The Treasury also expects to lose £1.15 billion in taxes over five years due to the decision and has said it will pay for this by increasing the tax on online gambling from 15% to 21%, raising £1.225 billion over the same period.

Wright said the delay was not just about giving bookmakers time to absorb the impact of FOBT curbs, but also to allow online operators to prepare for their increased tax burden.

A spokesperson for charity Christian Action Research and Education (Care) said: 'This all looks like there has been a dodgy backroom deal done with the bookies at the expense of communities and problem gamblers that will lose out with this delay. The idea that bookies need more time to prepare is simply absurd when weighed up against the profits that they will bank because of this delay.'

1 November 2018

Greyhound welfare boosted through multi-million pound deal with gambling industry

Bookmakers agree additional payments worth up to £3 million in a positive step which will ensure a fair return to the sport from industry giants.

By Department for Digital, Culture, Media & Sport and Mims Davies MP

Thousands of racing greyhounds are to be better cared for as a result of a new deal worth an estimated £3 million this year, to be paid for by some of Britain's biggest bookmakers.

The Minister for Sport, Mims Davies has announced that the funding will contribute towards new tailored training for veterinary staff, the expansion of an injury recovery scheme to ensure more greyhounds can enjoy a full and active life following racing, and the provision of more homes for dogs as they enter retirement, through increased funding for the Greyhound Trust.

The extra money will also go towards improving safety across the nation's 21 licensed racetracks, kennel improvements and the provision of air-conditioning for trainers' vehicles to improve welfare standards.

The voluntary commitment from Betfred, William Hill, Sky Betting and Gaming, and Paddy Power Betfair, was reached following discussions chaired by the Department for Digital, Culture, Media & Sport, which called for a fair return to the greyhound industry from bookmakers' profits on the sport.

This follows major operators Ladbrokes-Coral, Bet 365 and Jennings Bet who have previously made commitments on the same basis.

The move will be underpinned by the 'Greyhound Commitment' – a long-term strategic plan from the Greyhound Board of Great Britain, which will ensure animal welfare and the integrity of greyhound racing remain paramount in the sport.

Sport Minister, Mims Davies, said:

'I am delighted to have reached an agreement with leading operators to ensure the welfare of our greyhounds is protected and improved through this fund.

'As the sixth most watched sport in Britain, it is clear that the welfare and care of all racing greyhounds, from registration to retirement, must be a fundamental part of its successful future.

'I strongly urge all remaining bookmakers that take bets on greyhound racing who have not signed up to this agreement to follow suit and support the sport.

'Any greyhounds put to sleep due to medical treatment being too expensive, or a poor prognosis, is one too many – we must stop this.'

Mark Bird, Managing Director of the Greyhound Board of Great Britain, said:

'The Greyhound Board are extremely grateful for the conclusion of the mediation and the commitment of the major bookmakers to contribute additional funds from their on-line businesses.

'The GBGB has outlined clear ambitions, within our "Greyhound Commitment" as to where this new income will be spent, with the majority supporting greyhound welfare standards and initiatives, both throughout their racing careers but also as part of their homing process following retirement from the sport.'

Joe Scanlon, Chairman of the British Greyhound Racing Fund, said:

'With this deal the BGRF will be close to full support from all the major retail and online operators and it will provide a firm basis for delivering the enhanced welfare and integrity provision the sport of greyhound racing expects.

'This agreement would not have been possible without the support of the Minister and her team at DCMS, Lord Lipsey, who has worked tirelessly to improve the welfare of greyhounds over many years and of course the major bookmakers for their continued support of the Fund.'

The agreement took effect from 1 January 2019 and is expected to increase the income to the British Greyhound Racing Fund to around £10 million a year.

10 January 2019

How to tackle problem gambling

An article from **The Conversation.**

THE CONVERSATION

By Mark Griffiths, Director of the International Gaming Research Unit and Professor of Behavioural Addiction, Nottingham Trent University.

At the Labour Party conference, the party's deputy leader Tom Watson said that if they formed the next government they would introduce legislation to force gambling operators to pay a levy to fund research and NHS treatment to help problem gamblers deal with their addiction. This is something which I wholeheartedly support and is also something that I have been calling for myself for over a decade.

The most recent statistics on gambling participation by the Gambling Commission in August 2017 reported that 63% of the British population had gambled in the last year and that the prevalence rate of problem gambling among those aged 16 years and over was 0.6%–0.7%. While this is relatively low, it still equates to approximately 360,000 adult problem gamblers and is of serious concern.

At present, the gambling industry voluntarily donates money to an independent charitable trust (GambleAware) and most of this money funds gambling treatment, with the remaining monies being used to fund education and research. In the 12 months prior to March 2017, the gambling industry had donated £8 million, an amount still 20% below the £10 million a year I recommended in a report I wrote for the British Medical Association a number of years ago.

A statutory levy of 1% on all gambling profits made by the British gambling industry would raise considerably more money for gambling education, treatment and research than the £8m voluntarily donated last year and is the main reason why I am in favour of it.

A public health matter

Gambling has not been traditionally viewed as a public health matter. However, I believe that gambling addiction is a health issue as much as a social issue because there are many health consequences for those addicted to gambling, including depression, insomnia, intestinal disorders, migraine, and other stress-related disorders. This is in addition to other personal issues, such as problems with personal relationships (including divorce), absenteeism from work, neglect of family and bankruptcy.

There are also many recommendations that I would make in addition to a statutory levy. These include:

⇨ Brief screenings for gambling problems among participants in alcohol and drug treatment facilities, mental health centres and outpatient clinics, as well as probation services and prisons should be routine.

⇨ The diagnosis and effective treatment of gambling problems must be addressed within GP training.

Furthermore, GPs should screen for problem gambling in the same way that they do for other consumptive behaviours, such as cigarette smoking and alcohol drinking. At the very least, GPs should know where they can refer their patients with gambling problems.

⇨ Research into the efficacy of various approaches to the treatment of gambling addiction in the UK needs to be undertaken and should be funded by GambleAware.

⇨ Treatment for problem gambling should be provided under the NHS (either as standalone services or alongside drug and alcohol addiction services) and funded by gambling-derived revenue – for example, a 'polluter pays' model.

⇨ Education and prevention programmes should be targeted at adolescents along with other potentially addictive and harmful behaviours, such as smoking, drinking and drug taking, within the school curriculum.

Growing awareness

Problem gambling is very much a health issue that needs to be taken seriously by all in the medical profession. General practitioners routinely ask patients about smoking and drinking, but gambling is something that is not generally discussed. Problem gambling may be perceived as a grey area in the field of health. But if the main aim of practitioners is to ensure the health of their patients, then an awareness of gambling and the issues surrounding it should be an important part of basic knowledge in the training of those working in the health field.

Gambling is not an issue that will go away. Opportunities to gamble and access to gambling have increased due to the fact that anyone with Wi-Fi access and a smartphone or tablet can gamble from wherever they are. While problem gambling can never be totally eliminated, the Government must have robust gambling policies in place so that potential harm is minimised for the millions of people who gamble. For the small minority of individuals who develop gambling problems, there must be treatment resources in place that are affordable and easily accessible.

11 October 2017

Help for problem gambling

Being a compulsive gambler can harm your health and relationships, and leave you in serious debt.

If you have a problem with gambling and you'd like to stop, support and treatment is available.

Are you a problem gambler?

Try this questionnaire:

⇨ Do you bet more than you can afford to lose?

⇨ Do you need to gamble with larger amounts of money to get the same feeling?

⇨ Have you tried to win back money you have lost (chasing losses)?

⇨ Have you borrowed money or sold anything to get money to gamble?

⇨ Have you wondered whether you have a problem with gambling?

⇨ Has your gambling caused you any health problems, including feelings of stress or anxiety?

⇨ Have other people criticised your betting or told you that you had a gambling problem (regardless of whether or not you thought it was true)?

⇨ Has your gambling caused any financial problems for you or your household?

⇨ Have you ever felt guilty about the way you gamble or what happens when you gamble?

Score 0 for each time you answer 'never'
Score 1 for each time you answer 'sometimes'
Score 2 for each time you answer 'most of the time'
Score 3 for each time you answer 'almost always'

If your total score is 8 or higher, you may be a problem gambler.

Help for problem gamblers

There's evidence that gambling can be successfully treated in the same way as other addictions. Cognitive behavioural therapy usually has the best results.

Treatment and support groups are available for people who want to stop gambling:

GamCare offers free information, support and counselling for problem gamblers in the UK. It runs the National Gambling Helpline (0808 8020 133) and also offers face-to-face counselling.

National Problem Gambling Clinic If you live in England or Wales, are aged 16 or over and have complex problems related to gambling, you can refer yourself to this specialist NHS clinic for problem gamblers.

Gordon Moody Association The Gordon Moody Association offers residential courses for men and women who have problems with gambling – email help@gordonmoody.org. uk or call 01384 241292 to find out more.

It also runs the Gambling Therapy website, which offers online support to problem gamblers and their friends and family.

Gamblers Anonymous UK runs local support groups that use the same 12-step approach to recovery from addiction as Alcoholics Anonymous. There are also **GamAnon** support groups for friends and family.

Self-help tips for problem gamblers

Do:

⇨ pay important bills, such as your mortgage, on payday before you gamble

⇨ spend more time with family and friends who don't gamble

⇨ deal with your debts rather than ignoring them – visit the National Debtline website for tips.

Don't:

⇨ view gambling as a way to make money – try to see it as entertainment instead

⇨ bottle up your worries about your gambling – talk to someone

⇨ take credit cards with you when you go gambling.

For more self-help tips, see the Royal College of Psychiatrists website.

If you're affected by someone's gambling

If you're having problems because of another person's gambling, it's best to be honest with them about it. They need to know how their behaviour is affecting you.

Support is also available to people who are worried about someone else's gambling:

GamCare

Gamcare offers support and information for partners, friends and family of people who gamble compulsively.

GamAnon

Local support groups for anyone affected by someone else's gambling problem.

31 December 2017

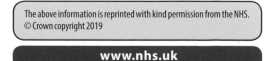

www.nhs.uk

Gambling ads must have serious addiction warnings, demand MPs

Crackdown would hold British betting firms to standards of tobacco industry.

By Michael Savage, policy editor

Gambling companies should be treated like tobacco firms and forced to display prominent health warnings about the potential harms of betting, according to a cross-party group of MPs and peers concerned about rising levels of addiction.

They call for gambling to be treated as a public health issue, with companies forced to drop suggestions that betting is 'fun' rather than harmful. A ban on gambling ads during live sporting events should be imposed because it allows bookmakers to reach young viewers before the watershed, they warn.

The group, which includes shadow culture secretary Tom Watson and former Tory minister John Hayes, states that the current regime in which 'the onus of social responsibility remains subject to the self-regulation of the licensee is not working'. It says that rules around betting ads are being flouted by the gambling industry, claiming that loopholes in the law mean they are doing so 'without fear of meaningful sanction'.

The number of over-16s who have a problem with gambling is thought to have risen by a third in three years, with about 430,000 sufferers in 2015. The plea comes after the Government announced its intention to tackle fixed-odds betting terminals, dubbed the 'crack cocaine' of gambling, by reducing the maximum stake from £100 to £2.

However, the cross-party group – which criticises ads, such as those run by Bet365 featuring actor Ray Winstone, which promote 'in game' betting – wants ministers to go further. In an open letter to culture secretary Matt Hancock, it demands sweeping measures to ensure 'greater compliance, fairness and social responsibility in the advertising and licensing of gambling'. Politicians including Watson, Hayes and former Lib Dem minister Don Foster, as well as the lord bishop of St Albans, have put their names to a series of proposals to tighten the rules on gambling companies, drawn up by the ResPublica thinktank. The proposals would see Britain take a similar approach to that in New Zealand, where gambling policy is handled by the Department of Health.

A chief demand is to treat the gambling industry like big tobacco. 'Gambling advertising should be consistent with other types of addictive or harmful products to public health such as cigarette packs, by featuring clearly identifiable health warnings that cannot be absorbed into an advert's overall design. The wording of gambling advertisements is a problem because words such as "win" and "fun" are emphasised rather than "harm", thus normalising the idea of gambling as a leisure pursuit rather than an addiction.'

The group also asks for a clampdown on rules that allow bookmakers to show ads during live matches and events: 'The current exception to the watershed that permits gambling adverts during live sporting events needs to be closed.

'Echoing a range of voices including the Church of England, we've found that this loophole both undermines the principle of the watershed and poses a risk of harm to young people – particularly young men and at-risk gamblers.

'We think the only way of closing the current loophole is a comprehensive ban on gambling advertising during live sporting events, including TV ads, billboard ads and clothing sponsorship.'

They also criticised the practice of 'affiliate marketing', which has seen adverts disguised as news articles used to direct people to betting sites, and tipsters allowed to earn commission by recommending long-shot bets unlikely to pay off. Affiliates are agencies paid to drive gamblers to online casinos and bookmakers.

The group calls for companies to be threatened with having their licences revoked should they be found to benefit from the practice.

The gambling industry is self-regulating, but has faced criticism after a string of failings. Last year online betting company 888 was fined £7.8 million after more than 7,000 people who had voluntarily banned themselves from gambling were still able to access their accounts. Last week online company Sky Bet was fined £1 million for allowing hundreds to keep betting after they asked to be barred from doing so.

Watson said: 'Gambling addiction is Britain's hidden epidemic. It's time to start treating this as the public health crisis it is.'

A spokeswoman for the Department for Culture, Media & Sport said: 'As well as reducing the maximum FOBT stake to £2, we have set out a package of measures to increase protections around online gambling and advertising. From next month, responsible gambling messages must appear on screen throughout all television gambling adverts, and a multimillion-pound safer gambling advertising campaign will launch later this year.'

27 May 2018

In numbers

33,611
Number of fixed odds terminals in the UK in 2017.

£1.8 billion
Total collected by bookmakers (after payouts) from FOBTs in 2016/17. Income from all betting was £13.8 billion.

106,236
People employed in the gambling industry.

Barclays is now letting customers block payments to gambling companies

It's the first mainstream finance company to do so, following in the footsteps of challenger bank Monzo

By Liam Geraghty

Barclays has launched a feature that will let customers turn off payments to certain retailers in a bid to protect the UK's problem gamblers.

The new tool allows people to block transactions at supermarkets, restaurants, takeaways, bars and petrol stations as well as bookmakers and gambling sites.

Premium rate websites and phone lines can also be blocked by pressing a button on Barclays mobile banking app.

The financial giant is not the first to offer the service – challenger bank Monzo introduced it in the summer in a bid to 'prevent financial problems caused by gambling, rather than trying to support people once they've already happened'.

But Barclays is the first mainstream bank to make the move, hoping to protect the UK's 340,000 problem gamblers and 1.7 million people at risk of racking up thousands of pounds in debt and putting them at risk of damaging their mental health.

Catherine McGrath, managing director at Barclays, said: 'We are always looking for new ways to support our customers and make it easier for them to manage their finances. This new control feature is the latest new service that we have introduced in the Barclays Mobile Banking app that aims to give all of our customers a better way to manage their money in a simple, secure and effective way.'

The tool was developed in conjunction with advisors from the Money Advice Trust and based on research from the Money and Mental Health Policy Institute.

'Technology that meets everyday banking needs, while recognising the challenges many of us face in our lives, is the way forward,' said Chris Fitch, vulnerability lead at the Money Advice Trust. 'Giving everyone more control is the key to achieving this – whether this is someone who wants to be less vulnerable to fraud, or a customer who is trying to take charge of their gambling.'

11 December 2018

Premier League football clubs should do more to tackle gambling addiction, says NHS chief

'Taxpayers should not be left to pick up the pieces,' says Simon Stevens.

By Harriet Agerholm

Premier league football clubs must do more to tackle gambling addiction, the head of NHS England Simon Stevens has said.

The chief executive described compulsive gambling as one of the 'new threats' facing the NHS and warned the already overstretched health service is being left to 'pick up the pieces' from gambling-related mental health issues.

Reports foreign gambling problems were 'failing to play their part' in funding treatment for the public health issue were 'deeply concerning', he told a conference in Manchester.

Although betting companies who reap profits in Britain are encouraged to contribute a total of £10 million to addiction treatments, a number of firms who sponsor Premier League clubs have yet to pay up this financial year, according to a July report in the *The Sunday Times*.

Speaking at the Health and Care Innovation Expo, Mr Stevens said: 'There is an increasing link between problem gambling and stress, depression and other mental health problems.

'Doctors report that two-thirds of problem gamblers get worse without help and the NHS does offer specialist treatment.

'But reports that foreign gambling companies are failing to play their part in co-funding help for addicts are deeply concerning.

'Taxpayers and the NHS should not be left to pick up the pieces; the health of the nation is everyone's responsibility.

'The NHS will now work with the Premiership on how we persuade these foreign gambling companies to do the right thing.'

Mr Stevens said the NHS needs to get 'more serious about aspects of prevention in public health, including what you might call "the new public health"', with an estimated 430,000 people in the UK dealing with a gambling problem.

'One of the things, if we're serious about prevention, that we need to do – we need to be getting on to the Premier League and asking them to ensure that those foreign gambling firms are playing their part,' he told the audience.

Around 370,000 11–16-year-olds spent their money on gambling in the course of one week in England, Scotland and Wales, according to a report published by the Gambling Commission last year.

The regulator estimated that 25,000 were problem gamblers.

5 September 2018

Why healthcare services have a problem with gambling

An article from **The Conversation.**

THE CONVERSATION

By Sean Cowlishaw, Research Fellow in Primary Health Care, University of Bristol

'I have a problem with gambling. There's not enough of it.'

That was the admission from billionaire Steve Wynn, a major figure in the casino industry, speaking at a recent gambling research conference in (where else?) Las Vegas. And sure, it made for a good quote. But it's also a rather glib dismissal of a serious issue that affects many thousands of people across the world.

The UK certainly has a problem with gambling. At least it has since 2007, when laws were changed to allow for huge growth in gambling opportunities and exposure. It has been hard to ignore the subsequent explosion in industry advertising, which increased by around 500% between 2007 and 2013. By contrast, you may have missed the increased numbers of high-intensity electronic gambling machines, called Fixed-Odds Betting Terminals (FOBTs), which now occupy the high street (within betting shops) and allow punters to wager up to £100 every 20 seconds.

Yet Britain doesn't have much insight into its problem with gambling. Compared to most other addictive behaviours, involving drugs or alcohol for example, gambling is largely ignored by health services and public health agencies. This is partly because gambling is a hidden concern. It does not manifest with physical warning signs. Indicators are usually visible in extreme cases only, and generally following major life crises such as extreme debt or relationship breakdown.

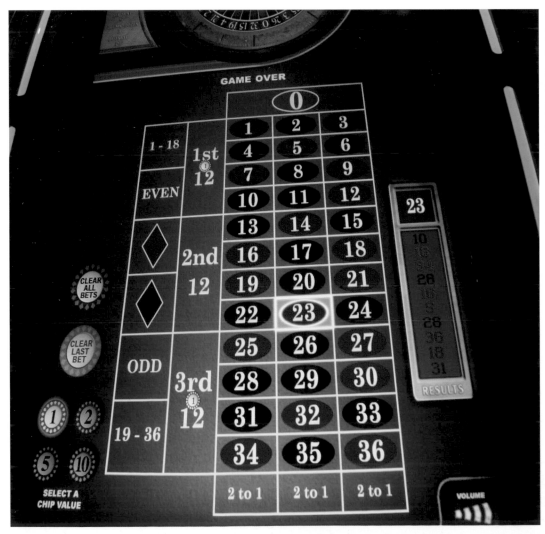

On top of this, the gambling industry has a surprisingly direct role in funding a great deal of the research into gambling, directly and indirectly through a third party organisation called GambleAware. It therefore plays a significant part in determining what we know about the nature of problems and possible solutions.

But people with gambling problems account for large amounts of industry revenue (up to 60% in dog racing). And this creates a clear conflict of interest for the gambling industry. Any success in reducing gambling problems is likely to reduce profits too.

So what of general practice, which is usually the first point of a contact with the healthcare system? Does it

have a problem with gambling? Our recent research suggests it does. In a study of more than 1,000 patients in waiting rooms of general practices in the south-west of England, around one in 20 patients reported at least some degree of gambling problem. These levels were higher among young males and patients showing signs of depression or risky drinking. Around 7% of respondents reported problems among family members and were also likely to experience harms from gambling.

The findings suggest an issue for primary care that is hidden from healthcare providers. Gambling problems are strongly linked with poor mental health, suicidal tendencies and serious consequences for families through relationship problems and domestic violence. Gambling problems also create difficulties for the broader community through overuse of healthcare services. Primary care has important roles in responding to many such health concerns, including other addictive behaviours such as smoking and alcohol misuse and complex psycho-social issues such as domestic violence – it could have similar involvement in improving help-seeking and intervention for people with gambling problems.

Responding to a hidden addiction

There's much more we need to know before we can determine the best ways in which general practice can help respond to gambling problems. There are different ways of identifying people who would benefit from help or intervention, such as universal screening or 'case-finding' by

questioning of patients demonstrating visible risk. Clinical responses can also vary and range from brief advice to onward referral. These may lead to very different equations in terms of the costs of interventions, including burdens on practitioners, and the balance of these compared to potential benefits.

In the absence of much attention to the health risks of gambling – and a lack of independent funding for research and interventions – it seems unlikely that there will be rapid progress in responding to gambling problems in general practice. But there is a need now for practitioners to be vigilant and inquire about potential problems. This is particularly important among young males or patients showing signs of depression, risky drinking or drug use, and financial difficulties.

As we've seen, the problem with gambling is that these issues are hidden from view. They have not been a priority when compared to health concerns that are more visibly obvious, such as obesity and alcohol misuse. GPs and practice nurses have an important part to play in putting these problems on the healthcare agenda.

13 June 2017

⇨ In November 2018 the Gambling Commission, which regulates gambling providers, revealed that 1.7% of children are classed as having a gambling problem. (page 4)

⇨ 14% – equivalent to 450,000 – children aged 11 to 16 bet regularly, more than have taken drugs, smoked or drunk alcohol. (page 4)

⇨ In government, the Department for Digital, Culture, Media & Sport is responsible for gambling. (page 4)

⇨ The introduction of the National Lottery in 1994 paved the way for the 2005 Gambling Act. Once the act came into force in 2007, gambling was more visible through open advertising; putting it online made the activity even more prominent and available. (page 6)

⇨ 600% increase in gambling advertising on TV since the 2005 Gambling Act came into force in 2007. (page 6)

⇨ On average, online gamblers have four accounts with online gambling operators. 6% of online gamblers have bet on eSports during the past 12 months, with rates highest among 25–34-year-olds. (page 10)

⇨ The PPF (Professional Players Federation) published alarming research which found professional sportspeople were three times more likely than the general public to develop a gambling problem. (page 12)

⇨ According to a recent report by the Gambling Commission, more than two million people in the UK are either problem gamblers or at risk of addiction. (page 13)

⇨ Almost half of Premier League clubs (nine) now have a betting firm as their shirt sponsor, with 16 teams in the Championship and League One having similar deals. (page 13)

⇨ 95 per cent of television advertising breaks during live UK football matches feature at least one gambling advert. (page 13)

⇨ According to a 2018 YouGov consumer research study 14% of Brits (around seven million people) took part in a World Cup sweepstake with their friends, family or workplace, including almost a quarter (24%) of full-time workers. (page 14)

⇨ A Gambling Commission audit due for release reveals that the number of problem gamblers aged 11 to 16 rose to 55,000 over two years. It also found that 70,000 youngsters were at risk and that 450,000 children bet regularly, the equivalent of one in seven children aged 11 to 16. (page 15)

⇨ Gambling Commission research found about 450,000 children gamble on a weekly basis. About 9,000 of those were described as 'problem gamblers'. (page 16)

⇨ After a decade of bombarding children with gambling adverts – 80% have seen them on TV and 70% through social media – 370,000 of 11–16-year-olds now gamble, starting at an average age of just 12. (page 17)

⇨ 27% of children aged 13–18 have heard of skin gambling. (page 19)

⇨ Of all those children who have heard of skin gambling, 36% have gambled skins. (page 19)

⇨ 46% of children across the UK aged 13–17 say they are able to access 18+ websites if they want.   (page 20)

⇨ The British public loses around £1.8 billion each year betting on FOBTs (fixed odds betting terminals). (page 28)

⇨ Around 370,000 11–16-year-olds spent their money on gambling in the course of one week in England, Scotland and Wales, according to a report published by the Gambling Commission last year. (page 37)

⇨ In a study of more than 1,000 patients in waiting rooms of general practices in the south-west of England, around one in 20 patients reported at least some degree of gambling problem. These levels were higher among young males and patients showing signs of depression or risky drinking. (page 39)

Bingo

A game in which players mark off numbers on cards as the numbers are drawn randomly by a caller, the winner being the first person to mark off all their numbers.

Bookmaker

A bookmaker's job is to take bets, calculate odds and pay out money when someone wins a bet.

Casino

A casino is an entertainment venue where various forms of gambling are offered. Casinos may include tables for games such as poker and roulette, as well as fruit machines. Bets are placed with chips (small plastic discs used to represent money). Chips can be bought and exchanged for money on entering and leaving the casino.

Fixed Odds Betting Terminal (FOBT)

An electromechanical device that allows people to bet on the outcome of a game or event with fixed odds. FOBTs have been highly criticised for their potential to develop addiction among players and have even been called the 'crack cocaine' of gambling. In response to this, in 2014, the Association of British Bookmakers introduced the facility for players to set a limit on the time they wish to play and the money they wish to spend.

Fruit machine

Fruit or slot machines are often found in pubs and casinos. Players insert money and are required to match symbols (usually fruit) in order to win the jackpot.

Gambling

An activity in which one or more persons take part, where a 'stake' (most often money) is placed on the result of an event whose outcome is uncertain. Examples include betting on sporting events, lotteries, bingo or card games.

Gambling Commission

The regulatory authority for gambling in the UK. The Gambling Commission was set up under the Gambling Act 2005, as an independent non-departmental public body to assist with compliance and enforcement of UK gambling licensing regulations. It is supported by the Department for Culture, Media & Sport.

Loot box

In video games, a loot box is an in-game purchase consisting of a virtual container that awards players with items and modifications based on chance. Part of the issue is in the way games unlock content, encouraging what is basically gambling through loot boxes.

Lottery

A lottery is a form of gambling based purely on chance. Numbers are drawn at random from a set range, and customers win if their pre-chosen numbers match the ones that are drawn. A fee is charged to enter the lottery and the jackpot is a percentage of the amount paid by entrants.

Online gambling

Placing bets or taking part in casino games over the Internet. Internet gambling can be more dangerous than traditional forms, as players are easily able to transfer large amounts of cash without leaving their home. Since the money is transferred electronically, it can seem less 'real' and debts build up more easily.

Pool betting

A betting pool is simply a form of gambling where people pay a fixed price to enter and then, once taxes and profits are removed, the remaining funds are shared amongst those who have made the correct predictions.

Problem gambling

When gambling becomes an addiction that starts to have a noticeable negative impact on someone's life, this is referred to as 'problem gambling'. It might affect relationships, employment or someone's financial situation: for example, they may acquire heavy debts, and the secretive nature of their addiction may put a strain on family relationships.

Remote gambling

Placing bets by remote means: for example, using a mobile phone or computer. The term 'remote' refers to the fact that players do not need to enter a bookmakers or casino to place their bet; they can gamble from any location

Skin gambling

Skins are virtual items that can be won or purchased within certain video games to decorate and customise weapons. They rarely affect gameplay and are mainly aesthetic but, due to their popularity, a marketplace has developed for the trading of skins.

Assignments

Brainstorming

⇨ Brainstorm what you know about gambling. Consider the following:

- What is gambling?
- What is problem gambling?
- What is skin gambling?
- What are loot boxes?
- What is a bookmaker?
- What are fixed-odds bets?

Research

⇨ Conduct a survey among the students in your year. Find out the following information:

- Have they ever placed a bet or taken part in any gambling activity?
- What kind of gambling activities do they pursue?
- How many gamble online?
- Does this differ between the genders?
- Write a short report of your findings and illustrate them with a graph or a pie chart.

⇨ In small groups, do some research into loot boxes. What are they? Do you think they are a form of gambling? Write a report which should cover one side of an A4 sheet.

⇨ In pairs, research online gambling in the UK. You should consider the types of gambling sites online and the age groups they are aimed at. Write a report, which should include an infogram.

⇨ In pairs, do some research into casinos in the UK. Ask your parents and their friends if they have ever visited a casino. Would they do so again? How much did they gamble and did they win or lose? Write a report on your findings.

⇨ Do some research into the effect gambling can have on people's lives. You should consider both the financial and social impact on people and the risk of becoming addicted. Write a report on your findings and feedback to your class.

Design

⇨ Design a leaflet to raise awareness of gambling amongst young people under the age of 18. You should include signs and symptoms of problem gambling and sources of help and advice.

⇨ Design an app that will help people who have a gambling problem. Your app could be a self-help guide or maybe something which would automatically cut-off a player's access to another app once they have spent a certain amount of money.

⇨ Design a poster to be displayed on school/college notice boards to raise awareness of under-age gambling.

⇨ In pairs, go through this book and discuss the cartoons you come across. Think about what the artists were trying to portray with each illustration.

⇨ Choose an article from this book and draw an illustration to highlight its key theme/message.

Oral

⇨ 'Designed to deceive: how gambling distorts reality and hooks your brain'. As a class discuss this statement and the reasons why you think people get hooked on gambling.

⇨ In pairs, discuss why you think there is an increase in the levels of gambling amongst young people. Feedback to your class.

⇨ In small groups, prepare a presentation that looks at the different aspects of gambling. You should consider the different types of gambling, the ages and sexes of people who participate and the reasons why they enjoy gambling.

⇨ Split the class into two groups. One group will argue in favour of gambling advertising and the other group will argue against.

Reading/writing

⇨ Imagine you are an agony aunt/uncle and have received a letter from a young boy who has a problem with gambling. He is spending all of his money from his Saturday job on gambling and has even taken money from his parents without their consent. He is worried sick they will find out and what the consequences will be. He wants to stop gambling but does not know how to. Write a suitable reply and give him information about where he might go to get help.

⇨ Write a letter to your school newspaper highlighting the issue of gambling amongst young people. You should give some facts about gambling. Use the article on page 10 to help you.

⇨ Write a one-paragraph definition of a 'loot box' and compare to that of a classmate.

⇨ Write an essay exploring gambling advertising. Do you think these ads should be banned? Your essay should cover at least one A4 side.

⇨ Write a blog about under-age gambling and explain why teenagers should not gamble at such a young age.

Acknowledgements

The publisher is grateful for permission to reproduce the material in this book. While every care has been taken to trace and acknowledge copyright, the publisher tenders its apology for any accidental infringement or where copyright has proved untraceable. The publisher would be pleased to come to a suitable arrangement in any such case with the rightful owner.

Images

All images courtesy of iStock except pages 8, 21, 22, 23, 26, 28, 30, 34, 35, 37 Pixabay. 12, 15, 16, 17, 24, 30, 39: Unsplash

Icons

Icons on pages 4, 6, 7 & 11 were made by Freepik, Pixel Buddha, pongsakornRed from www.flaticon.com.

Illustrations

Don Hatcher: pages 1 & 18. Simon Kneebone: pages 20 & 31. Angelo Madrid: pages 33 & 36.

Additional acknowledgements

With thanks to the Independence team: Shelley Baldry, Tina Brand, Danielle Lobban, Jackie Staines and Jan Sunderland.

Tracy Biram

Cambridge, January 2019